Best Editorial Cartoons of the Year

VIC HARVILLE
Courtesy Stephens Media Group

BEST EDITORIAL CARTOONS OF THE YEAR

2005 EDITION

Edited by
CHARLES BROOKS

PELICAN PUBLISHING COMPANY
Gretna 2005

Library of Congress Serial Catalog Data

Best Editorial Cartoons, 1972-
  Gretna [La.] Pelican Pub. Co.
      v. 30 cm annual-
"A Pictorial History of the Year."

1. United States—Politics and government—
1969—Caricatures—and Cartoons—Periodicals.
E839.5.B45 320.9'7309240207 73-643645
ISSN 0091-2220   MARC-S

Manufactured in the United States of America

Published by Pelican Publishing Company, Inc.
1000 Burmaster Street, Gretna, Louisiana 70053

Contents

Award-Winning Cartoons

2003 NATIONAL SOCIETY OF PROFESSIONAL JOURNALISTS AWARD
(Selected in 2004)

"NO DECISION HAS BEEN MADE..."

STEVE SACK

Editorial Cartoonist
Minneapolis Star-Tribune

Born in St. Paul, Minnesota; editorial cartoonist for *The Minnesota Daily,* 1978, the Fort Wayne, Indiana, *Journal Gazette,* 1979-81, and the Minneapolis *Star-Tribune,* 1981 to the present; co-producer of the children's Sunday comics feature "Professor Doodles"; also winner of National Headliner Award in 2003.

2004 PULITZER PRIZE

MATT DAVIES

Editorial Cartoonist
The Journal News (N.Y.)

Born in London, 1966; studied illustration and fine art at the Savannah College of Art and Design and the New York School of Visual Arts; editorial cartoonist for the Westchester County, New York, *Journal News;* cartoons syndicated by Tribune Media Services; also winner of the 2004 Herblock Award for editorial cartooning.

2004 HERBLOCK AWARD

MATT DAVIES

Editorial Cartoonist
The Journal News (N.Y.)

2003 SCRIPPS-HOWARD AWARD

(Awarded in 2004)

WALT HANDELSMAN

Editorial Cartoonist
Newsday

Born in 1957; graduated from the University of Cincinnati; editorial cartoonist for a chain of suburban Washington, D.C. weekly newspapers, 1982-85, the Scranton, Pennsylvania, *Times,* 1985-89; the New Orleans *Times-Picayune,* 1989-2001, and *Newsday,* 2001 to the present; author of five collections of editorial cartoons, as well as a children's book, published in 1995; also winner of the National Headliner Award, 1989 and 1983, the Society of Professional Journalists' Sigma Delta Chi Award, 1991, and the Pulitzer Prize, 1997.

2004 NATIONAL HEADLINER AWARD

US troops to be in Iraq longer than expected.

CLAY BENNETT

Editorial Cartoonist
The Christian Science Monitor

Born in Clinton, South Carolina, in 1958; graduated from the University of North Alabama in 1980; editorial cartoonist for the *St. Petersburg Times,* 1981-94, and *The Christian Science Monitor,* 1998 to the present; winner of the John Fischetti Award, 2001, the Sigma Delta Chi Award, 2001, the National Journalism Award, 2002, the Pulitzer Prize, 2002, and the National Headliner Award, 1999 and 2000.

2003 FISCHETTI AWARD
(Awarded in 2004)

JOHN COLE

Editorial Cartoonist
The Herald-Sun (N.C.)

Born in Rochester, New York, and reared in Lexington, Kentucky; graduated from Washington and Lee University in 1980; reporter for the Greenup, Kentucky, *News* and the Danville, Kentucky, *Advocate-Messenger;* graphics editor and editorial cartoonist for the *Durham Morning Herald* and the *Herald-Sun,* 1985 to the present; and author of *Politics, Barbecue & Balderdash,* published in 1995.

2004 BERRYMAN AWARD

ANN TELNAES

Editorial Cartoonist
Tribune Media Services

Born in Stockholm, in 1960; graduated from the California Institute for the Arts in 1984; animator and editorial cartoonist; winner of the National Headliner Award in 1997 and the Pulitzer Prize in 2001; cartoons syndicated by Tribune Media Services.

Best Editorial Cartoons of the Year

BILL GARNER
Courtesy Washington Times

14

Presidential Campaign

President George W. Bush won reelection after one of the nastiest, most hotly contested presidential campaigns in memory. The campaign drew passionate response from Democrats and Republicans alike, resulting in a record voter turnout.

Howard Dean led the Democrats' list of hopefuls until he imploded after a now-famous "screech" in a speech to supporters. His campaign lost momentum, and Massachusetts Sen. John Kerry quickly became the party choice. Kerry, who emphasized his military service in Vietnam, came under fire from veterans who had served in his unit.

In the book *Unfit for Command,* many of them claimed Kerry had lied about his military exploits and challenged his version of the circumstances surrounding his three Purple Heart medals. They also expressed outrage over Kerry's allegations of war crimes by American troops. Others who served on Kerry's swift boat praised the Democratic nominee's service.

Bush's National Guard service was questioned by critics, who contended that he did not always appear for duty when so ordered. The president produced records showing he had been honorably discharged.

ERIC SMITH
Courtesy Annapolis Capital-Gazette

15

JERRY BARNETT
Courtesy Indianapolis Star

WALT HANDELSMAN
Courtesy Newsday

JIM BORGMAN
Courtesy Cincinnati Enquirer

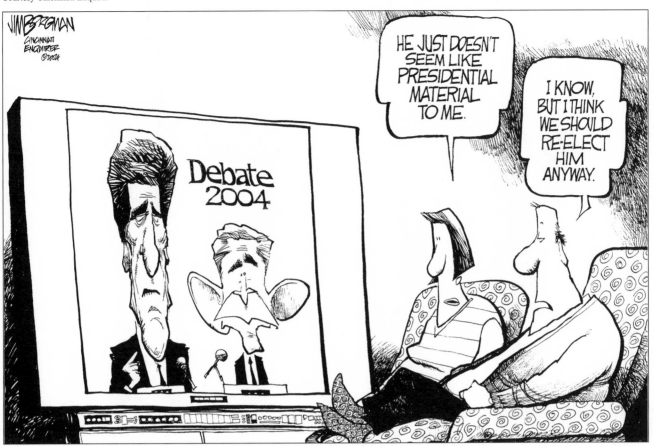

ROBERT ARIAIL
Courtesy The State (S.C.)

CHIP BECK
Courtesy The Real Washington

KERRY'S POST-GOP CONVENTION BOUNCE...

JIM LANGE
Courtesy Daily Oklahoman

ED GAMBLE
Courtesy Florida Times-Union

"HAD I BEEN READING TO CHILDREN AND HAD MY TOP AIDE WHISPERED IN MY EAR, 'AMERICA IS UNDER ATTACK,' I WOULD HAVE ACTED DIFFERENTLY..."

REX BABIN
Courtesy Sacramento Bee

CHRIS BRITT
Courtesy State Journal-Register

GRAEME MacKAY
Courtesy Hamilton Spectator

HOW the TERRORISTS PLAN to DISRUPT the ELECTION

SWIFT BOAT

MATT DAVIES
Courtesy The Journal News (N.Y.)

JOE R. LANE
Courtesy Denton Record-Chronicle

SCOTT-ALLEN PIERSON
Courtesy The Viking News

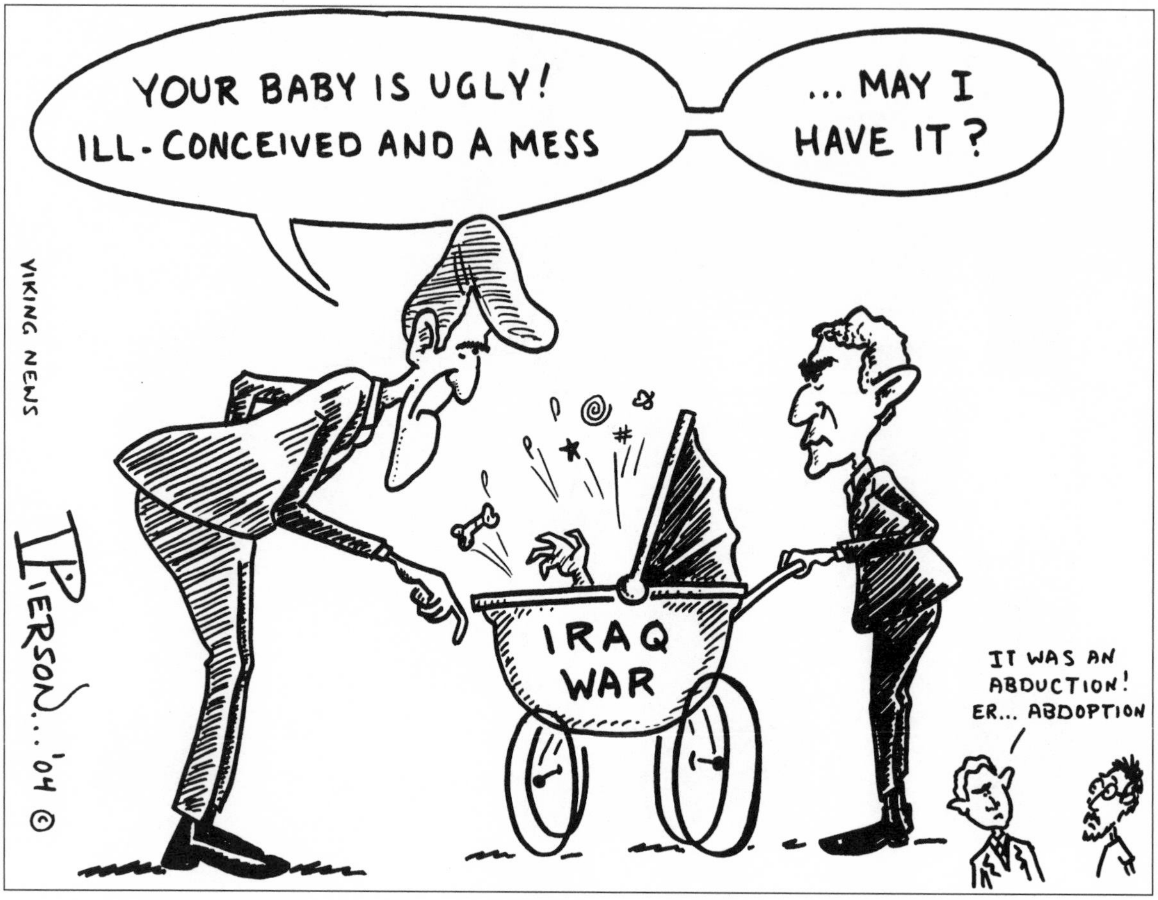
YOUR BABY IS UGLY! ILL-CONCEIVED AND A MESS
... MAY I HAVE IT?
VIKING NEWS
IRAQ WAR
IT WAS AN ABDUCTION! ER... ABDOPTION
PIERSON... '04 ©

KEVIN KALLAUGHER
Courtesy Baltimore Sun

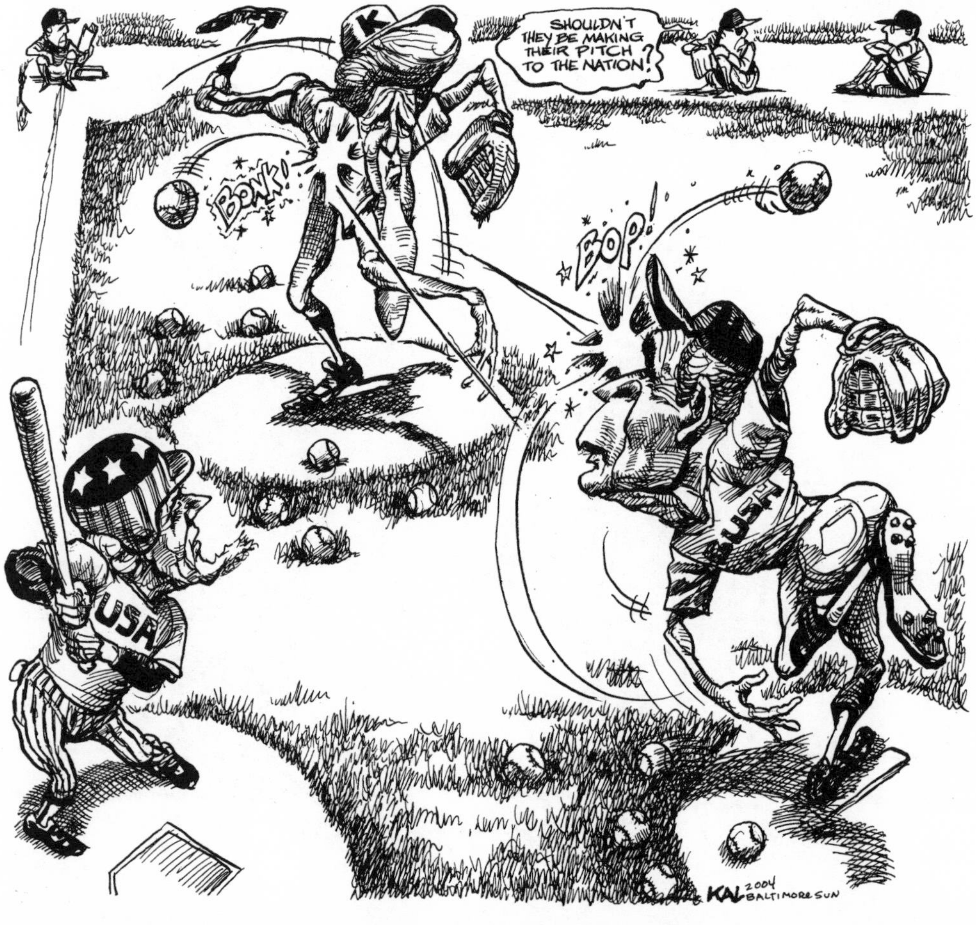
SHOULDN'T THEY BE MAKING THEIR PITCH TO THE NATION?
K
BONK!
BOP!
USA
BUSH
KAL 2004 BALTIMORE SUN

RANAN LURIE
Courtesy Cartoonews International Syndicate

STEVE BREEN
Courtesy San Diego Union-Tribune

THE ASS'S HORSE

CHIP BECK
Courtesy The Real Washington

LAZARO FRESQUET
Courtesy El Nuevo Herald

"Just think – after Nov. 2, we won't have to hear this any more."

"ARE WE THERE YET?"

GENE HERNDON
Courtesy Noblesville Daily Times

JOHN COLE
Courtesy The Herald-Sun (N.C.)

DAVID COX
Courtesy Arkansas Democrat-Gazette

JERRY BARNETT
Courtesy Indianapolis Star

JOE MAJESKI
Courtesy The Times-Leader (Pa.)

ANDREW WAHL
Courtesy Wenatchee World

MARK THORNHILL
Courtesy North County Times

JIM BORGMAN
Courtesy Cincinnati Enquirer

O'CONNOR
Courtesy Los Angeles Daily News

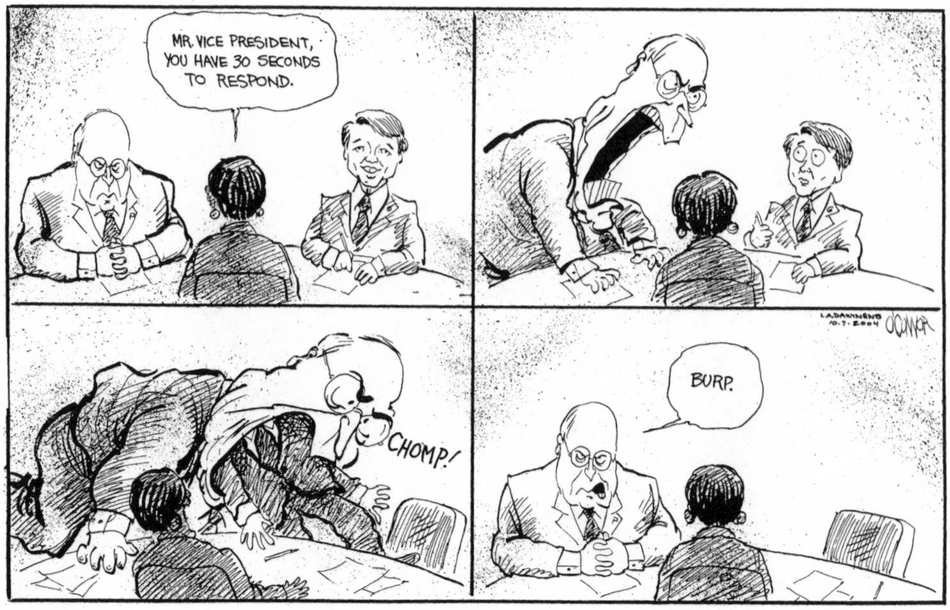
MR. VICE PRESIDENT, YOU HAVE 30 SECONDS TO RESPOND.
CHOMP!
BURP.
O'CONNOR

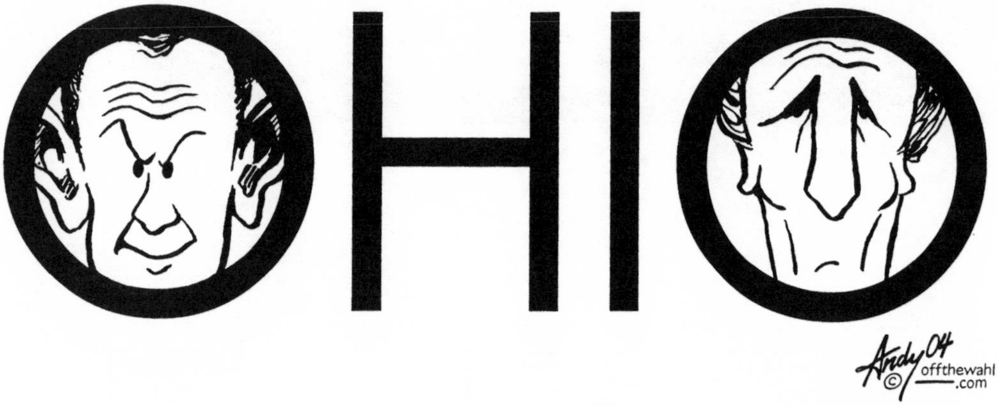
OHIO
Andy 04
© offthewahl.com

ANDREW WAHL
Courtesy Wenatchee World

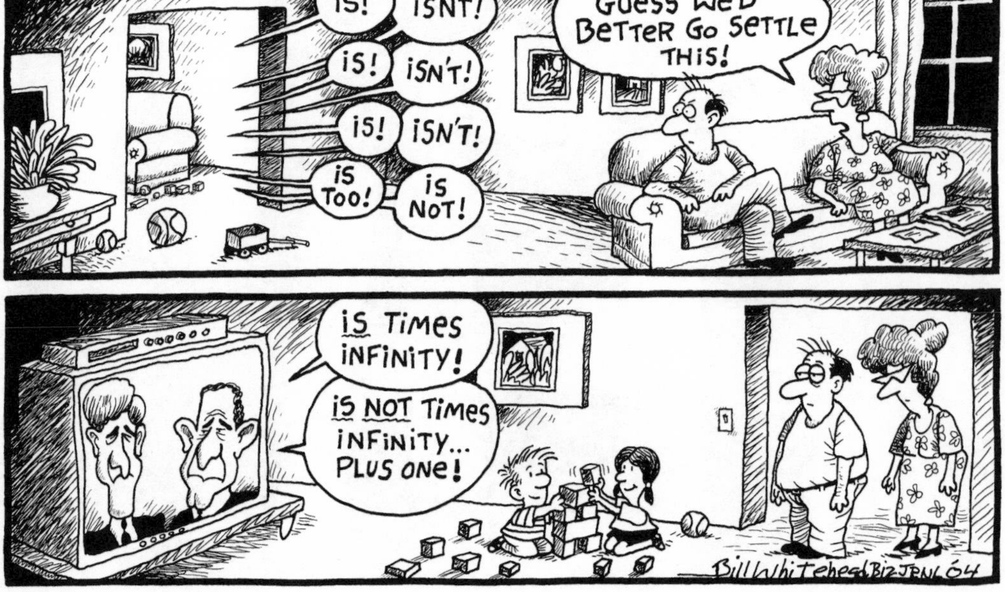
IS!
ISN'T!
IS!
ISN'T!
IS!
ISN'T!
IS TOO!
IS NOT!
GUESS WE'D BETTER GO SETTLE THIS!
IS TIMES INFINITY!
IS NOT TIMES INFINITY... PLUS ONE!
Bill Whitehead BizJrnl 04

BILL WHITEHEAD
Courtesy Kansas City Business Journal

MICHAEL RAMIREZ
Courtesy Los Angeles Times

JACK HIGGINS
Courtesy Chicago Sun-Times

VANCE RODEWALT
Courtesy Calgary Herald

Iraq / Terrorism

Although Iraqi dictator Saddam Hussein was captured near the end of 2003 following a tip from a relative, attacks against U.S. troops continued to escalate. Car bombings became commonplace, as did video-taped threats and decapitations of kidnapped foreigners, and huge stores of weapons were found. Train bombings by terrorists that killed 192 people persuaded the Spanish government to withdraw troops from Iraq. At year's end, Coalition troops were continuing to root out insurgents in Fallujah and Mosul in the face of stepped up attacks against Iraqi police.

Conceding that Iraq probably had no weapons of mass destruction, the Bush Administration accused Saddam and the United Nations of massive fraud and kickbacks—totaling billions of dollars—in the U.N. Oil for Food program. The program had been intended to curtail Iraq's war-making capability while providing food and medicine for Iraq's children. On June 28, Coalition forces turned over sovereignty to a provisional Iraqi government, and elections were scheduled for January 2005.

A commission studying the terrorist attacks of 9/11 issued a report critical of CIA intelligence efforts and a lack of cooperation between the CIA and the FBI. Congress responded, and in December passed the biggest overhaul of U.S. intelligence operations in fifty years.

MICHAEL RAMIREZ
Courtesy Los Angeles Times

THE CASE AGAINST SADDAM.

33

RANAN LURIE
Courtesy Cartoonews International Syndicate

ERIC SMITH
Courtesy Annapolis Capital-Gazette

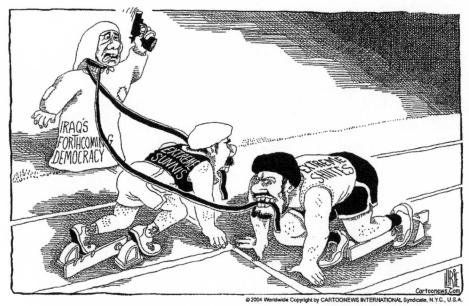

CHIP BOK
Courtesy Akron Beacon Journal

KEVIN KALLAUGHER
Courtesy Baltimore Sun

ROBERT ARIAIL
Courtesy The State (S.C.)

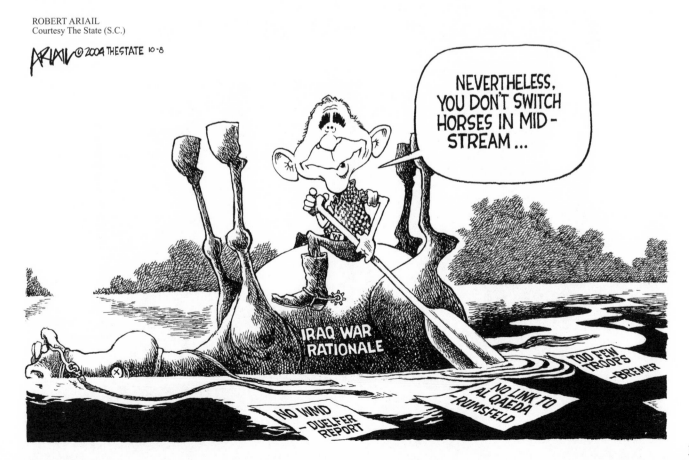

35

TOM STIGLICH
Courtesy Northeast Times

SAGE STOSSEL
Courtesy The Atlantic Monthly

BOB LANG
Courtesy Rightoons.com

MICHAEL RAMIREZ
Courtesy Los Angeles Times

DAVID COX
Courtesy Arkansas Democrat-Gazette

JOE MAJESKI
Courtesy The Times-Leader (Pa.

JACK JURDEN
Courtesy Wilmington News-Journal

JIM BUSH
Courtesy Providence Journal

ERIC SHANSBY
Courtesy Anniston Star

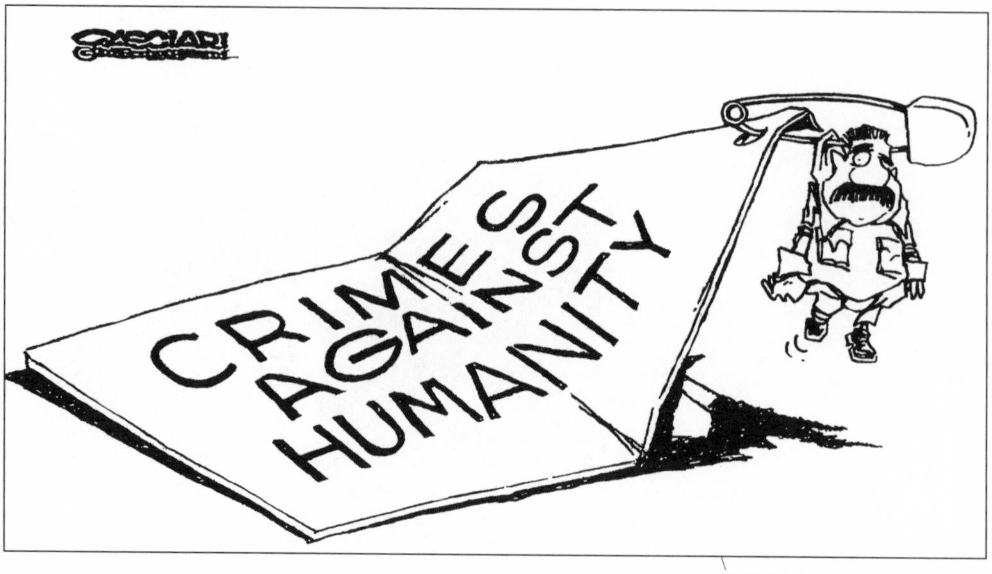
CRIMES AGAINST HUMANITY

JAMES CASCIARI
Courtesy Vero Beach Press-Journal

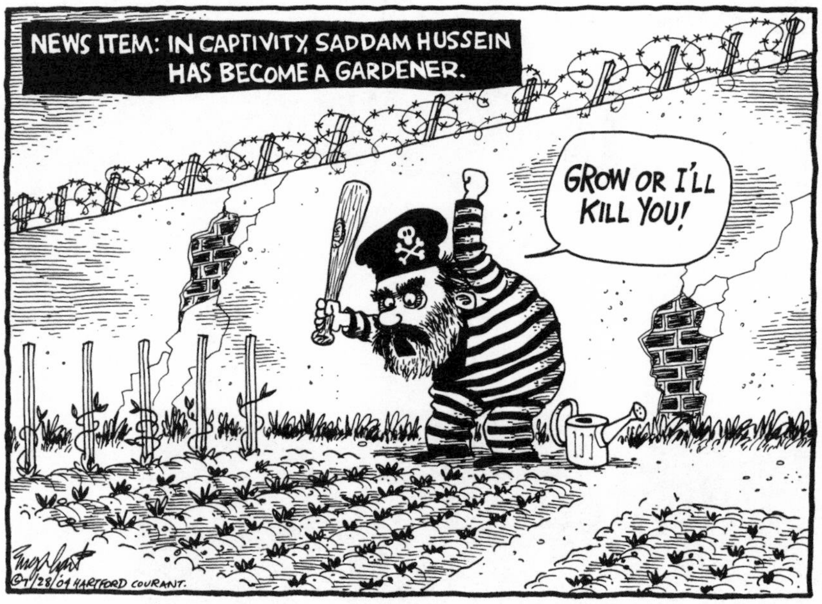
NEWS ITEM: IN CAPTIVITY, SADDAM HUSSEIN HAS BECOME A GARDENER.
GROW OR I'LL KILL YOU!

BOB ENGLEHART
Courtesy Hartford Courant

CLAY BENNETT
Courtesy Christian Science Monitor

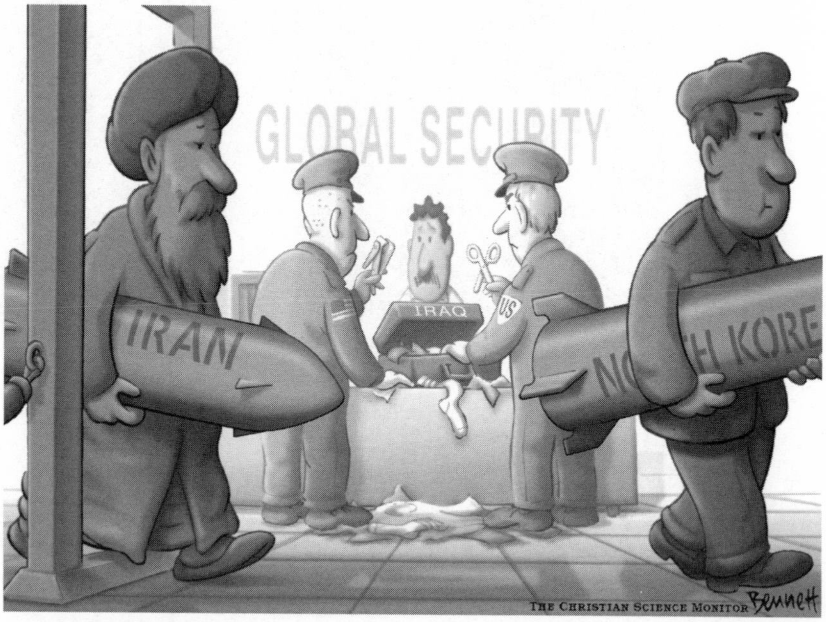
GLOBAL SECURITY
IRAQ
IRAN
US
THE CHRISTIAN SCIENCE MONITOR

JACK HIGGINS
Courtesy Chicago Sun-Times

JAMES McCLOSKEY
Courtesy The Daily News Leader (Va.)

LAZARO FRESQUET
Courtesy El Nuevo Herald

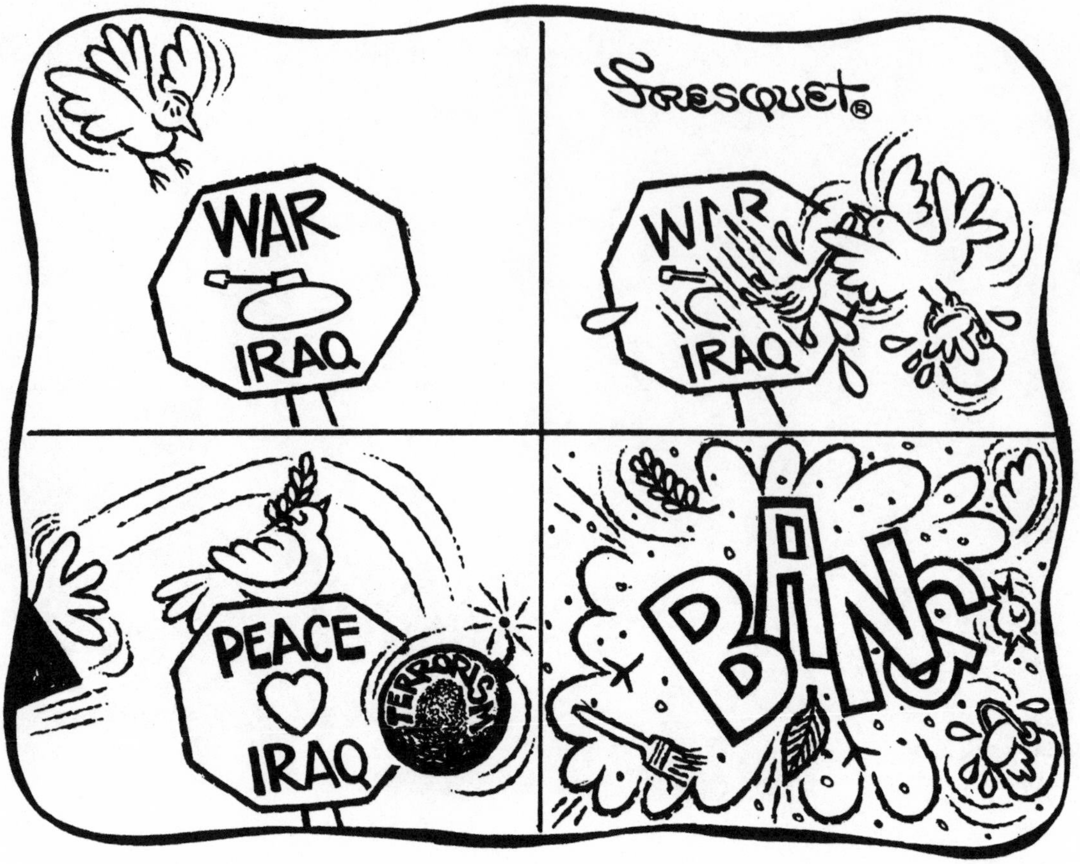

FRESQUET®
WAR
IRAQ
IRAQ
PEACE
IRAQ
TERRORISM
BANG

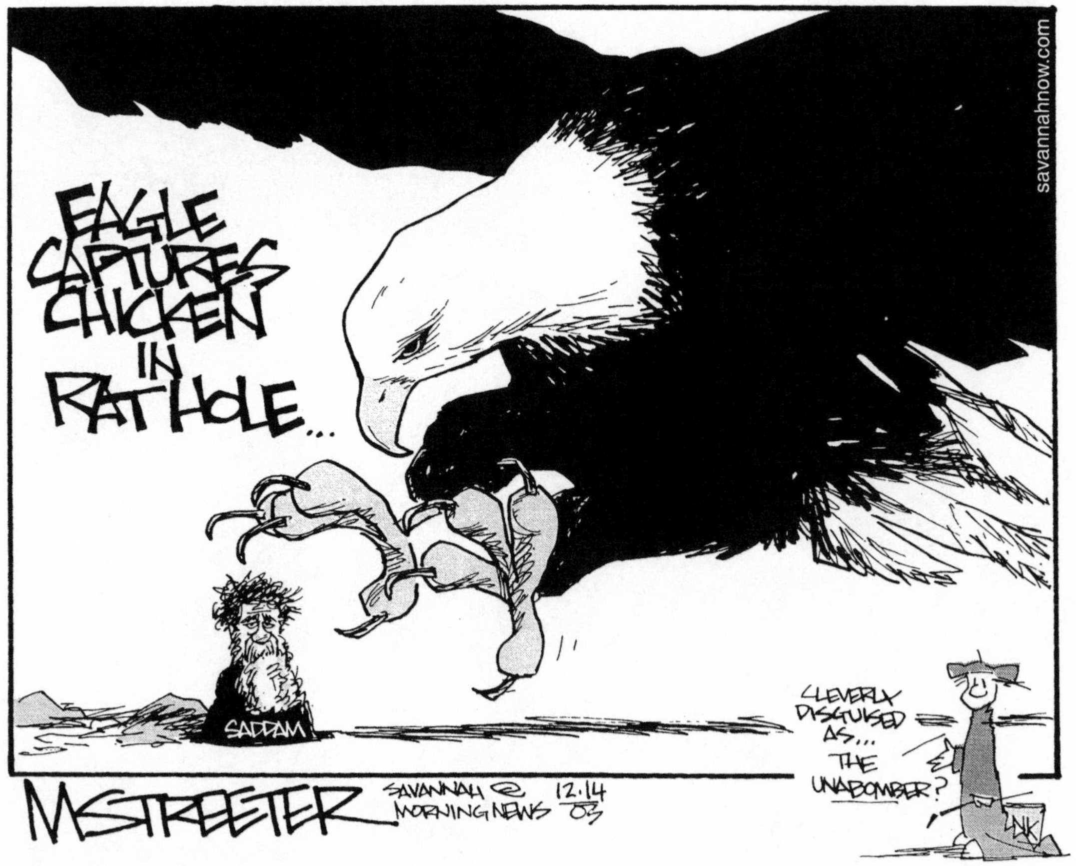

savannahnow.com
EAGLE CAPTURES CHICKEN IN RAT HOLE...
SADDAM
CLEVERLY DISGUISED AS... THE UNABOMBER?
MSTREETER
SAVANNAH MORNING NEWS
12.14 '03

MARK STREETER
Courtesy Savannah Morning News

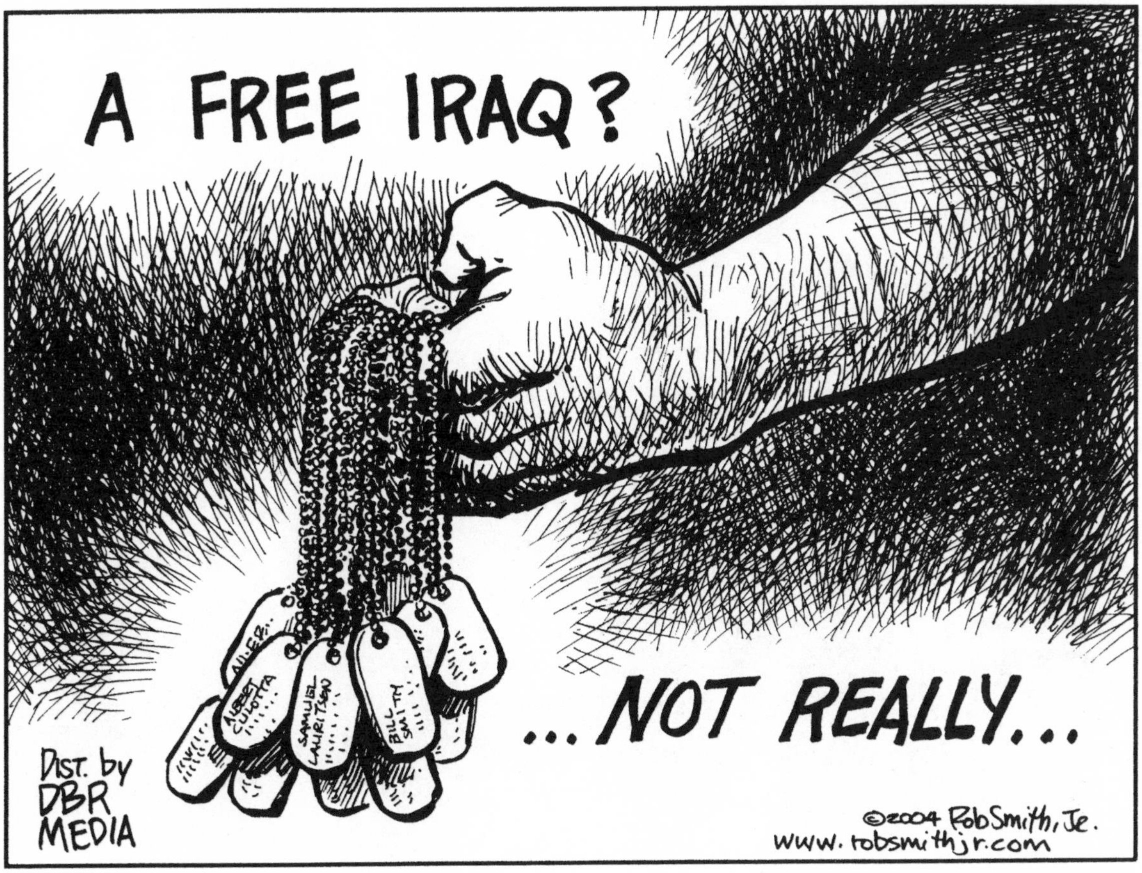
A FREE IRAQ?
...NOT REALLY...
Dist. by DBR MEDIA
©2004 RobSmith, Jr.
www.robsmithjr.com

ROB SMITH, JR.
Courtesy DBR Media

DANA SUMMERS
Courtesy Orlando Sentinel

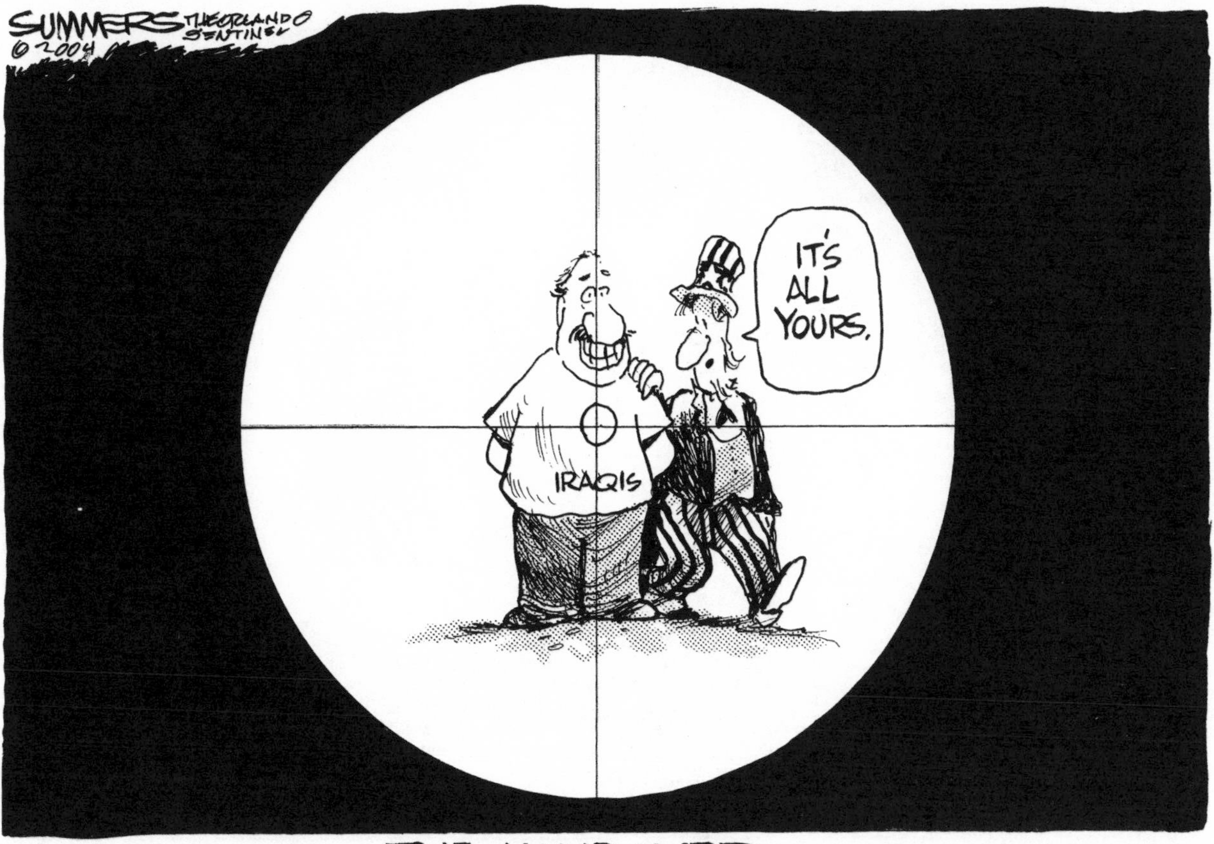
SUMMERS THE ORLANDO SENTINEL ©2004
IT'S ALL YOURS.
IRAQIS
THE HAND-OVER

MIKE SCOTT
Courtesy Newark Star-Ledger

RANAN LURIE
Courtesy Cartoonews International Syndicate

Expecting the newly-born Iraqi government

CLIFF LEVERETTE
Courtesy Magnolia Gazette

MICHAEL RAMIREZ
Courtesy Los Angeles Times

"AND THIS TIME IT VANISHED QUITE SLOWLY, BEGINNING WITH THE END OF THE TAIL, AND ENDING WITH THE GRIN, WHICH REMAINED SOME TIME AFTER THE REST OF IT HAD GONE..."

LINDA BOILEAU
Courtesy The State Journal (Ky.)

JIM BUSH
Courtesy Providence Journal

JACK CHAPMAN
Courtesy Desoto Times Today

DICK LOCHER
Courtesy Chicago Tribune

MIKE THOMPSON
Courtesy Detroit Free Press

STEVE KELLEY
Courtesy The Times-Picayune

ED STEIN
Courtesy Rocky Mountain News

JIM BORGMAN
Courtesy Cincinnati Enquirer

BOB LANG
Courtesy Rightoons.com

CHRIS BRITT
Courtesy State Journal-Register

MIKE LUCKOVICH
Courtesy Atlanta Journal-Constitution

CLAY BENNETT
Courtesy Christian Science Monitor

SCOTT STANTIS
Courtesy Birmingham News

STANTIS © 2004 THE BIRMINGHAM NEWS COPLEY NEWS SERVICE
BOY SCOUT
WE'RE BEING DEPLOYED TO HAITI.
AT LEAST WE CAN GET OUR NATION-BUILDING MERIT BADGE...
TROOPS, NATIONAL GUARD OVER-EXTENDED

MATT DAVIES
Courtesy The Journal News (N.Y.)

THE JOURNAL NEWS ©2004 MATT DAVIES 3/25
G.O.P. RALLYING CRY:
Q. WHERE WAS CLINTON IN THE WAR ON AL-QAIDA ??
WHITEWATER INVESTIGATION
LEWINSKY HEARINGS
A.

DANIEL FENECH
Courtesy Saline Reporter

DAVID COX
Courtesy Arkansas Democrat-Gazette

BRUCE PLANTE
Courtesy Chattanooga Times

52

MIKE LUCKOVICH
Courtesy Atlanta Journal-Constitution

CLAY BENNETT
Courtesy Christian Science Monitor

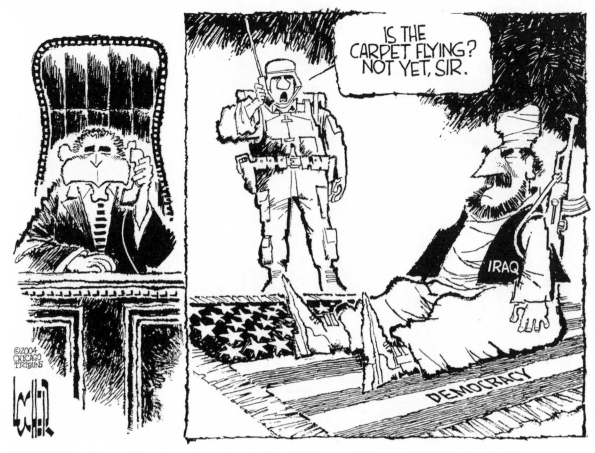

DICK LOCHER
Courtesy Chicago Tribune

JIM BORGMAN
Courtesy Cincinnati Enquirer

Bush Administration

Former White House counterterrorism czar Richard Clarke published a book that bitterly attacked President Bush's efforts to fight terrorism. Clarke, who had worked for four presidents, contended that Bush's decisions in reality had made the U.S. less secure against attack.

Another Bush appointee, former Treasury Secretary Paul O'Neill, issued a book of his own claiming that Bush had drawn up plans to invade Iraq long before the attacks of 9/11. He portrayed the president in staff meetings as "a blind man in a room full of deaf people."

Longtime CIA Director George Tenet resigned after continuing criticism of the Agency's shortcomings, and Defense Secretary Donald Rumsfeld came under attack for alleged prisoner abuses at Abu Ghraib in Iraq.

The economy made slow but steady progress, apparently boosted by President Bush's tax cuts. Everyone agreed that the 9/11 attacks had had a devastating effect on the economy, but the manufacturing sector continued to shed jobs because of improved technology and other efficiency boosters. Nevertheless, 1.3 million jobs were added during the year.

President Bush's National Guard record was assailed by CBS newsman Dan Rather, who later admitted that documents allegedly proving charges of Bush's absenteeism were forged.

Flash Flood!

JEFF DANZIGER
Courtesy Los Angeles Times Syndicate

"ONCE UPON A TIME, THERE WAS A BAD KING WHO LIVED IN IRAQ...."

PAUL CONRAD
Courtesy Los Angeles Times Syndicate

GEORGE DANBY
Courtesy Bangor Daily News

PETER DUNLAP-SHOHL
Courtesy Anchorage Daily News

MIKE PETERS
Courtesy Dayton Daily News

JEFF PARKER
Courtesy Florida Today

CHAN LOWE
Courtesy Fort Lauderdale News/
South Florida Sun Sentinel

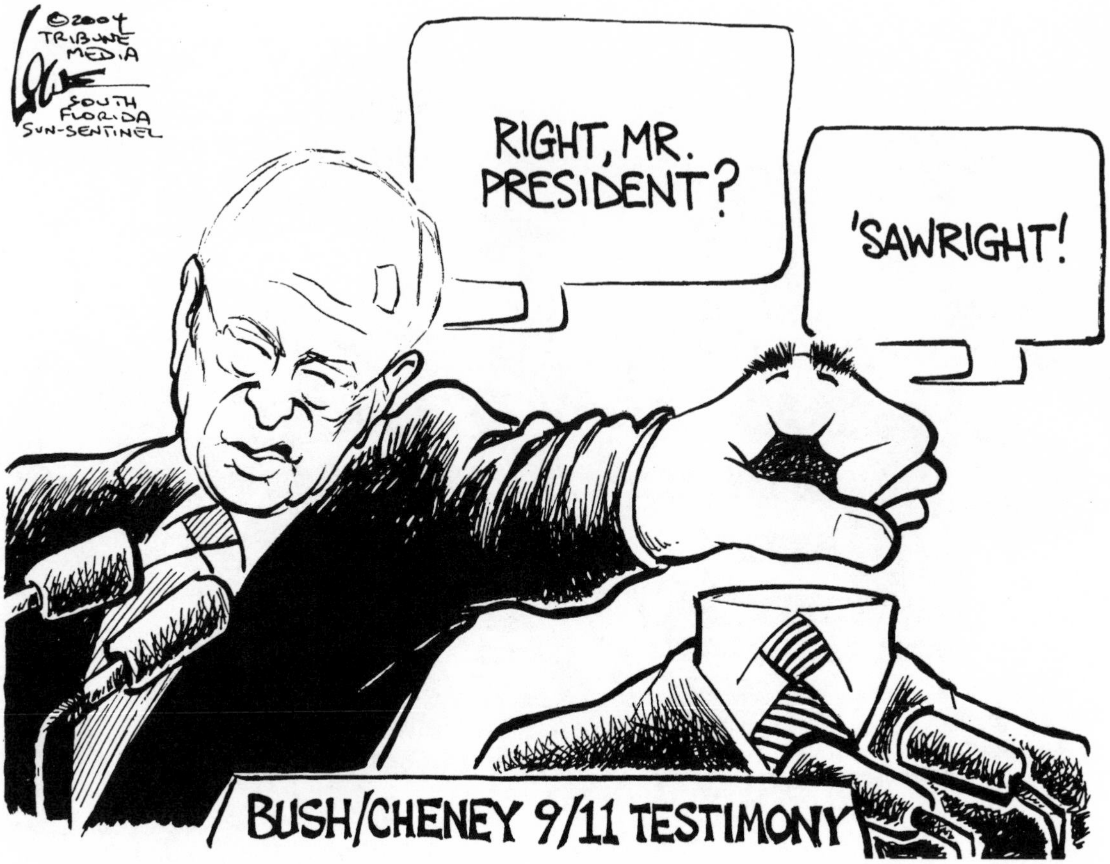
©2004 TRIBUNE MEDIA
LOWE
SOUTH FLORIDA SUN-SENTINEL
RIGHT, MR. PRESIDENT?
'SAWRIGHT!
BUSH/CHENEY 9/11 TESTIMONY

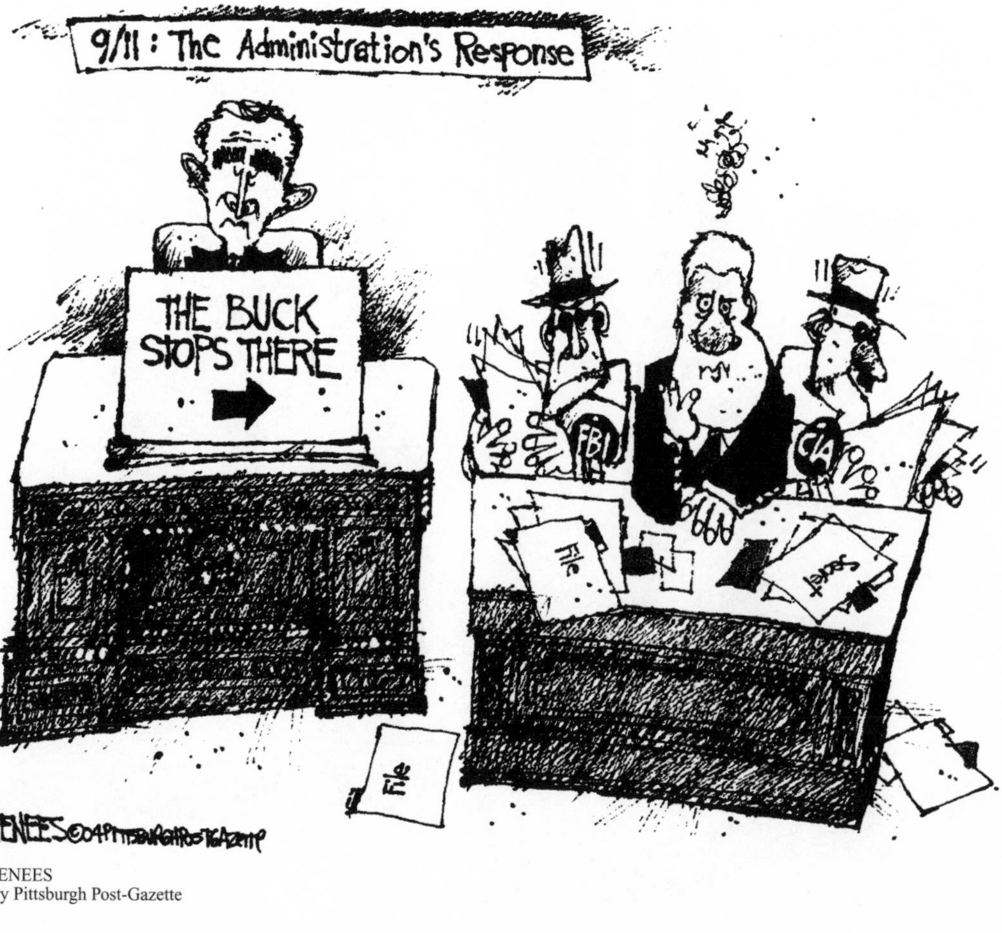
9/11 : The Administration's Response
THE BUCK STOPS THERE
FBI
CIA
File
Secret
File
TIM MENEES

TIM MENEES
Courtesy Pittsburgh Post-Gazette

ROB HARRIMAN
Courtesy Portland Tribune

WALT HANDELSMAN
Courtesy Newsday

59

BOB WIEGERS
Courtesy Rockford Register-Star

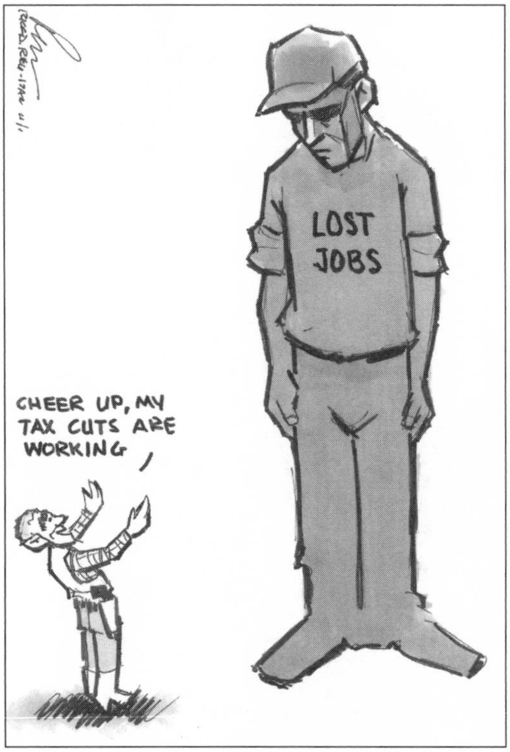
LOST JOBS
CHEER UP, MY TAX CUTS ARE WORKING

GRAEME MacKAY
Courtesy Hamilton Spectator

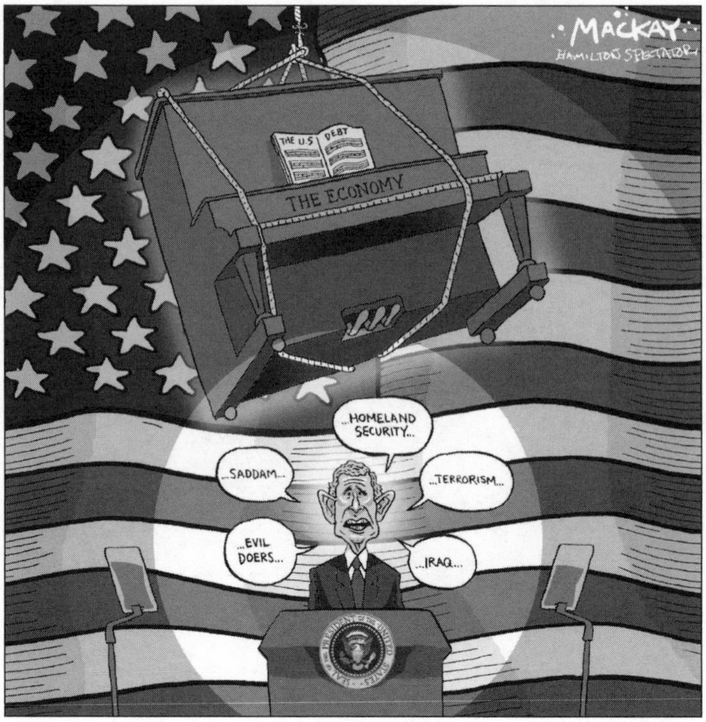
MACKAY HAMILTON SPECTATOR
THE U.S. DEBT
THE ECONOMY
...HOMELAND SECURITY...
...SADDAM...
...TERRORISM...
...EVIL DOERS...
...IRAQ...

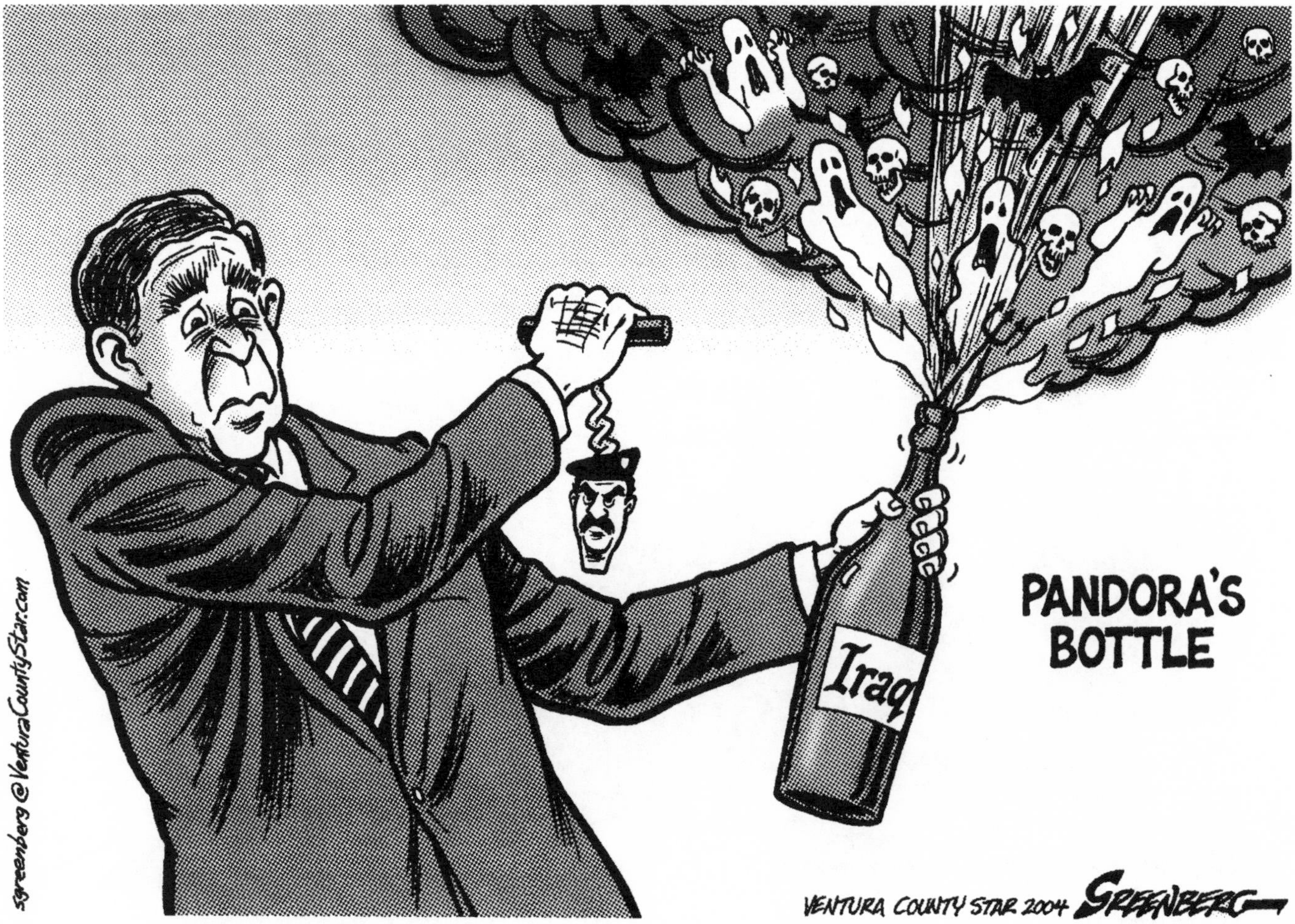
PANDORA'S BOTTLE
Iraq
sgreenberg@VenturaCountyStar.com
VENTURA COUNTY STAR 2004 GREENBERG

STEVE GREENBERG
Courtesy Ventura County Star

KEVIN KALLAUGHER
Courtesy Baltimore Sun

"...THE FINAL RESPONSIBILITIES OF ANY FAILURE IS MINE, AND MINE ALONE."

"SADDAM HUSSEIN IS RESPONSIBLE."

PAUL CONRAD
Courtesy Los Angeles Times Syndicate

STEVEN TEMPLETON
Courtesy Observer-Times

TIM BENSON
Courtesy Argus-Leader (S.D.)

MIKE LUCKOVICH
Courtesy Atlanta Journal-Constitution

HAP PITKIN
Courtesy Boulder Daily Camera

JOE HELLER
Courtesy Green Bay Press-Gazette

BRUCE BEATTIE
Courtesy Daytona Beach News-Journal

JOHN BRANCH
Courtesy San Antonio Express-News

STEVE SACK
Courtesy The Star-Tribune (Minn.)

THE PRESIDENT FINALLY LIFTS A FINGER IN REACTION TO THE ASSAULT WEAPONS BAN EXPIRING...

STEVEN LAIT
Courtesy Oakland Tribune

MIKE PETERS
Courtesy Dayton Daily News

ETTA HULME
Courtesy Fort Worth Star-Telegram

LINK FOUND BETWEEN IRAQ AND 9/11

ED HALL
Courtesy Baker County Press

BOB ENGLEHART
Courtesy Hartford Courant

MIKE KEEFE
Courtesy Denver Post

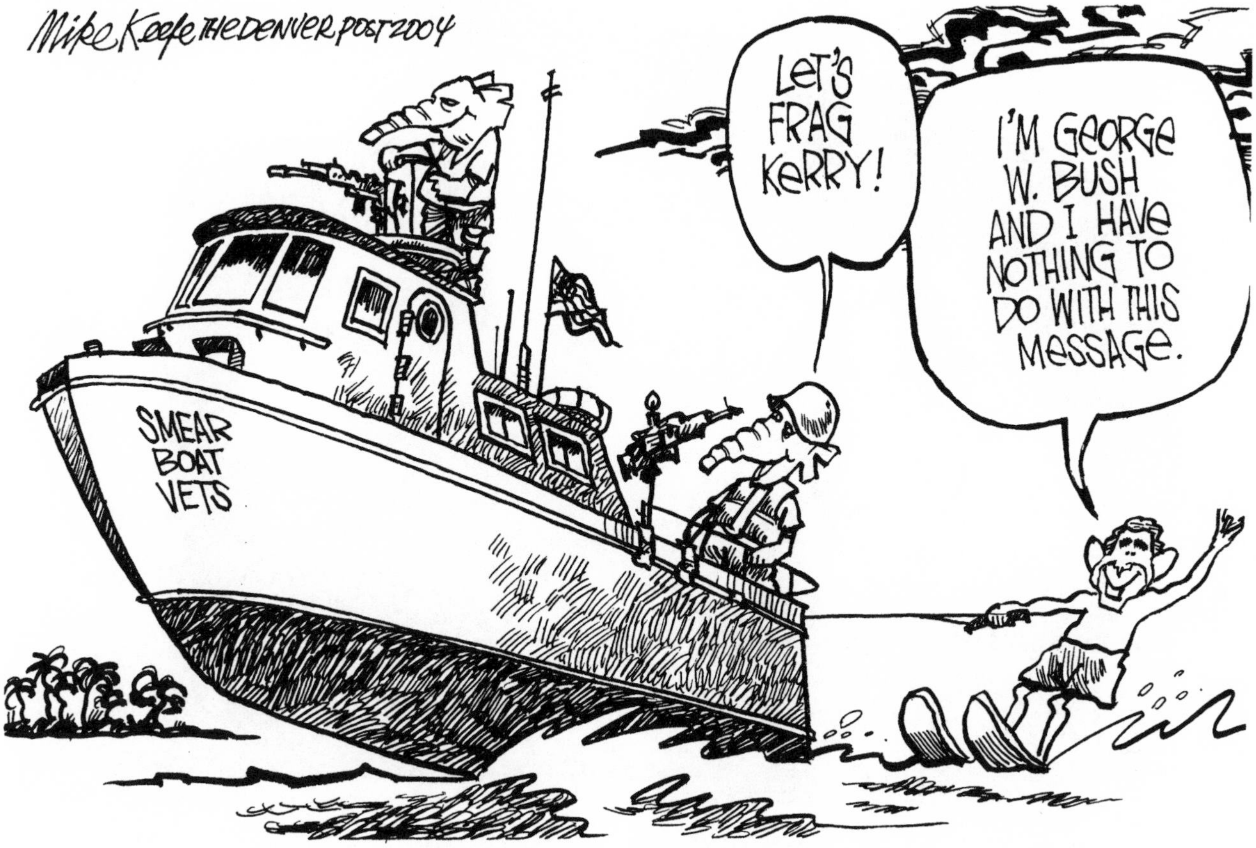
Mike Keefe THE DENVER POST 2004
LET'S FRAG KERRY!
I'M GEORGE W. BUSH AND I HAVE NOTHING TO DO WITH THIS MESSAGE.
SMEAR BOAT VETS

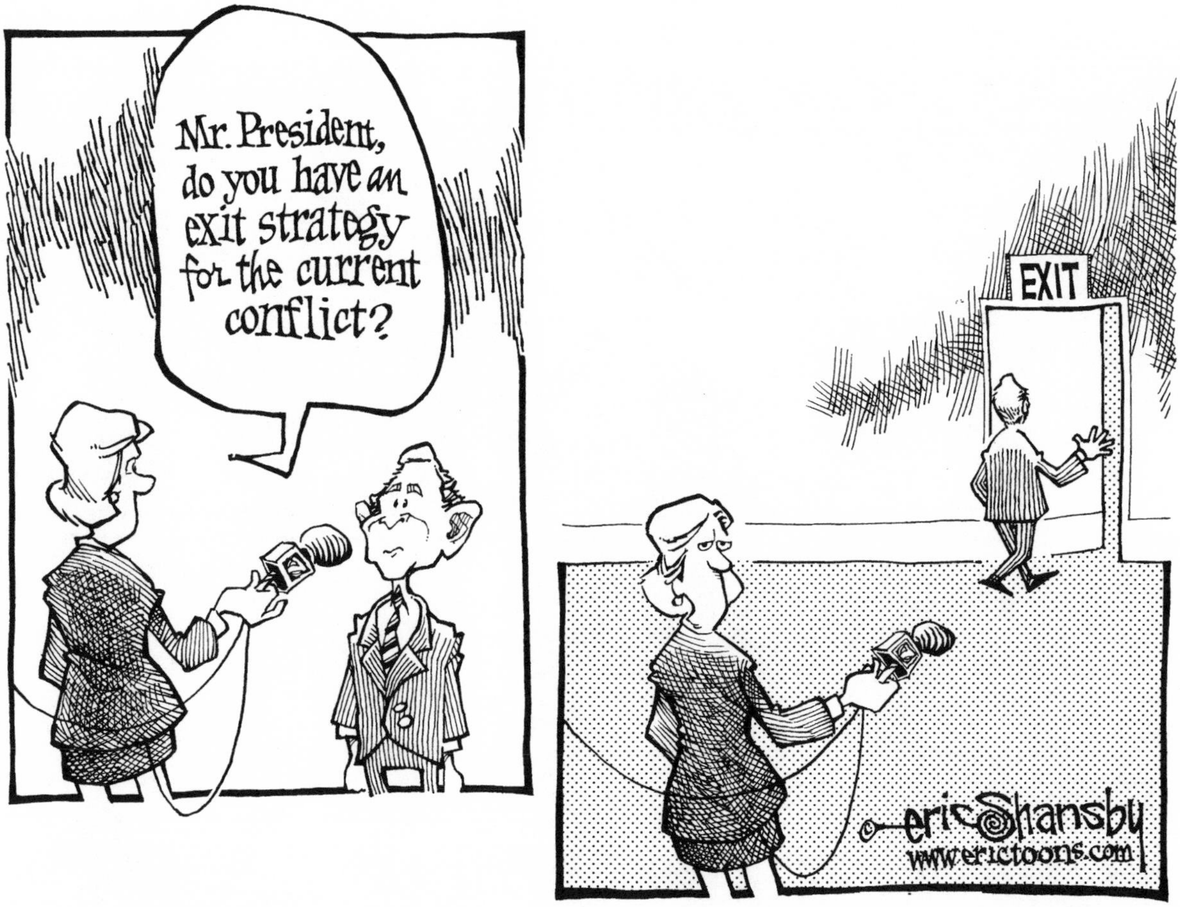
Mr. President, do you have an exit strategy for the current conflict?
EXIT
ericShansby
www.erictoons.com

ERIC SHANSBY
Courtesy Anniston Star

MICHAEL OSBUN
Courtesy Citrus County Chronicle

CLUELESS IN WASHINGTON

VANCE RODEWALT
Courtesy Calgary Herald

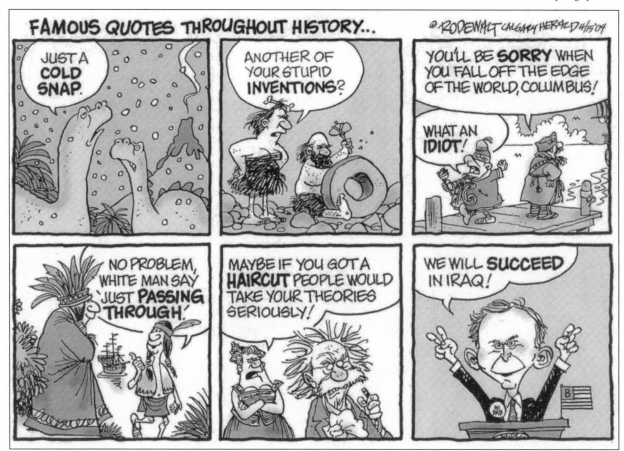

O'CONNOR
Courtesy Los Angeles Daily News

RICK KOLLINGER
Courtesy The Star-Democrat (Md.)

ANN CLEAVES
Courtesy Palisadian Post

RICHARD CROWSON
Courtesy Witchita Eagle

TONY BAYER
Courtesy News-Dispatch

STEVE SACK
Courtesy The Star-Tribune (Minn.)

SCOTT STANTIS
Courtesy Birmingham News

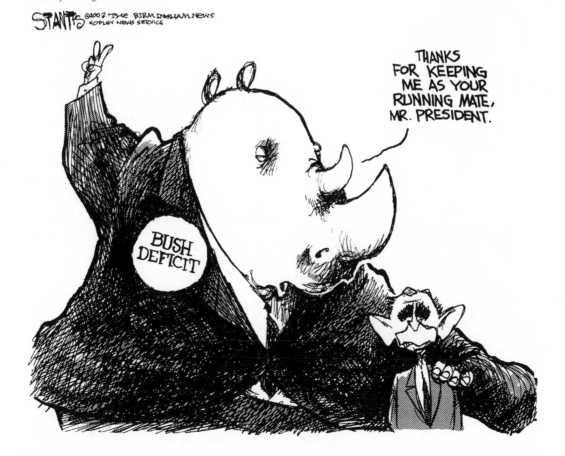

"I GUESS SMOKE AND MIRRORS IS THE ONLY WAY TO RUN A WAR."

THE WIND BENEATH MY WINGS....

CARL MOORE
Courtesy Creators Syndicate

Politics

Bankrolled by record spending, the fall elections produced unprecedented mudslinging and partisan attack ads. When the dust had settled, the Republicans had retained the White House and strengthened their hold on both houses of Congress.

The Democrats faced a variety of problems on the campaign trail, including Howard Dean's "screech" speech, Teresa Heinz Kerry's controversial comments, and John Kerry's perceived flip-flopping on the issues. Some felt that former President Bill Clinton, who underwent heart surgery during the campaign, had further upstaged Kerry with the publication of his autobiography, and Green Party candidate Ralph Nader threatened to siphon away Kerry voters. Moreover, the economy continued to improve—further bad news for the Democrats.

Democratic Sen. Zell Miller of Georgia, the keynote speaker at the Republican Convention, loudly endorsed President Bush for reelection and announced that he could not trust Democrat John Kerry with the nation's defense. Kerry replied that he had a plan for the war on terror but was vague on details.

Former Clinton advisor Sandy Berger was discovered exiting the National Archives with top-secret documents stuffed in his jacket and socks. The bizarre act was never explained.

STEVE McBRIDE
Courtesy Independence Daily Reporter

J. R. ROSE
Courtesy Byrd Newspapers

CARL MOORE
Courtesy Creators Syndicate

MICHAEL OSBUN
Courtesy Citrus County Chronicle

CONVENTION FOCUS

CHUCK ASAY
Courtesy Colorado Springs Gazette-Telegraph

PAUL FELL
Courtesy Lincoln Journal Star

SOMETHING YOU NEVER HEAR POLITICAL HOPEFULS
DISCUSS DURING THEIR CAMPAIGNS...

JOHN COLE
Courtesy The Herald-Sun (N.C.)

JIM LANGE
Courtesy Daily Oklahoman

PAUL NOWAK
Courtesy Scripps-Howard Newspapers

JOHN BRANCH
Courtesy San Antonio Express-News

GUY BADEAUX
Courtesy LeDroit

VAUGHN LARSON
Courtesy Wisconsin News-Press

MIKE LUCKOVICH
Courtesy Atlanta Journal-Constitution

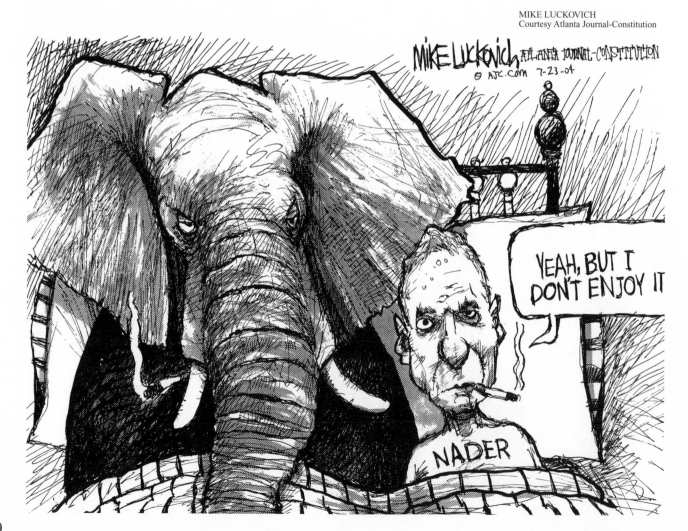

WAYNE STROOT
Courtesy Hastings Tribune

JAKE FULLER
Courtesy Gainesville Sun

82

STEVEN LAIT
Courtesy Oakland Tribune

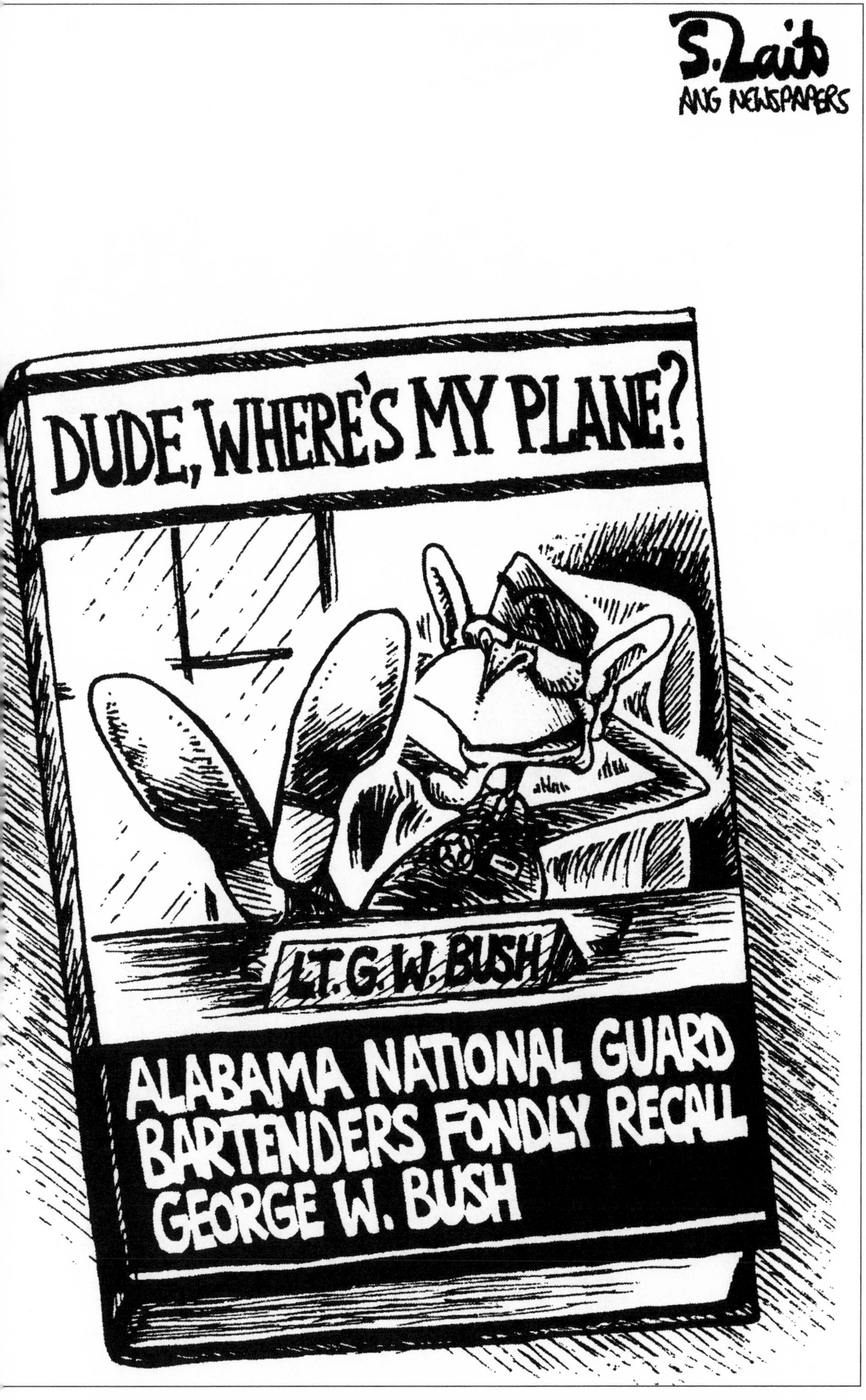
S. Lait
ANG NEWSPAPERS
DUDE, WHERE'S MY PLANE?
LT. G. W. BUSH
ALABAMA NATIONAL GUARD
BARTENDERS FONDLY RECALL
GEORGE W. BUSH

I DEMAND CREDIBILITY!
IRAQ WAR
TED
SO DO I
CHAPPAQUIDDICK

RANDY BISH
Courtesy Tribune-Review (Pa.)

ED GAMBLE
Courtesy Florida Times-Union

The clerics make the law in Iran, just like the Taliban did in Afghanistan and.....
....activist judges do now in the United States!
MASSACHUSETTS
CALIFORNIA
FLORIDA
GAMBLE

JIMMY MARGULIES
Courtesy The Record (N.J.)

It came and went quickly... but changed everything in its wake...
DEAN CAMPAIGN
MARGULIES
©2004 THE RECORD NEW JERSEY
www.northjersey.com/margulies

BILL MANGOLD
Courtesy Heritage Newspapers

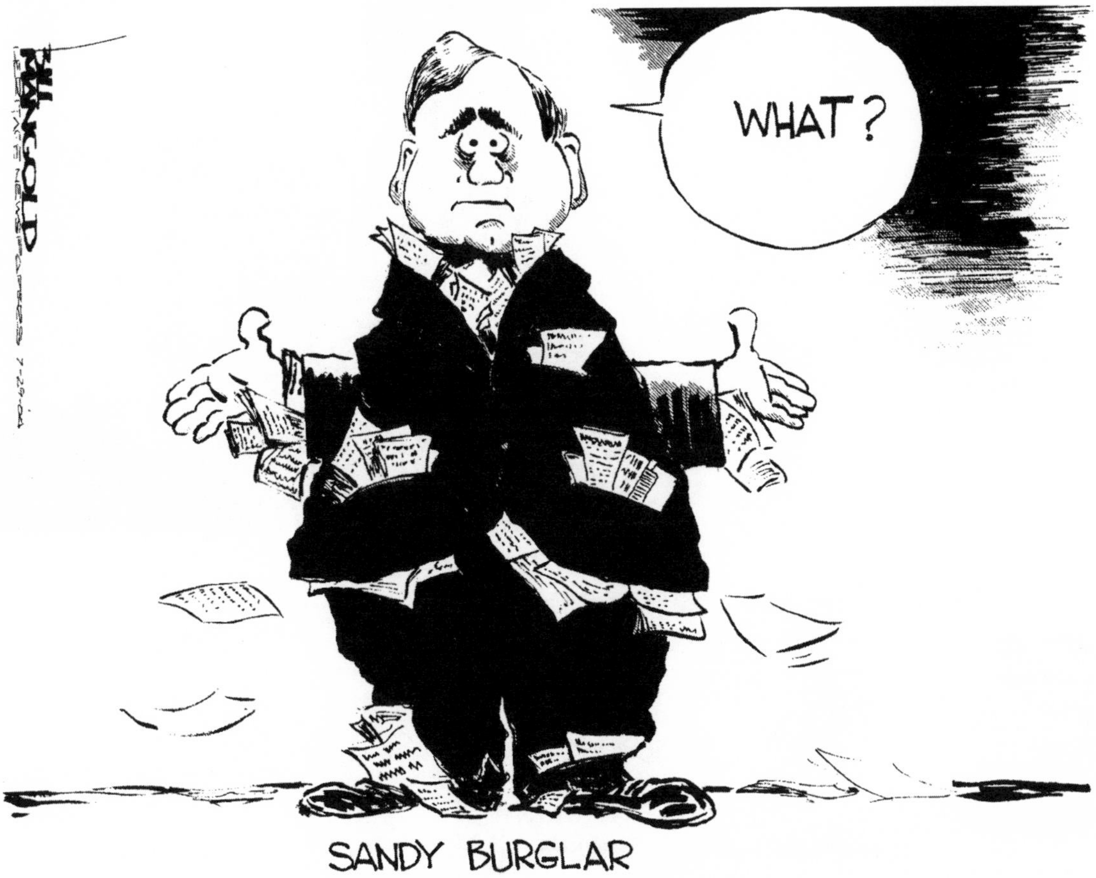

WHAT?
SANDY BURGLAR

DAVID HITCH
Courtesy Worcester Telegram and Gazette

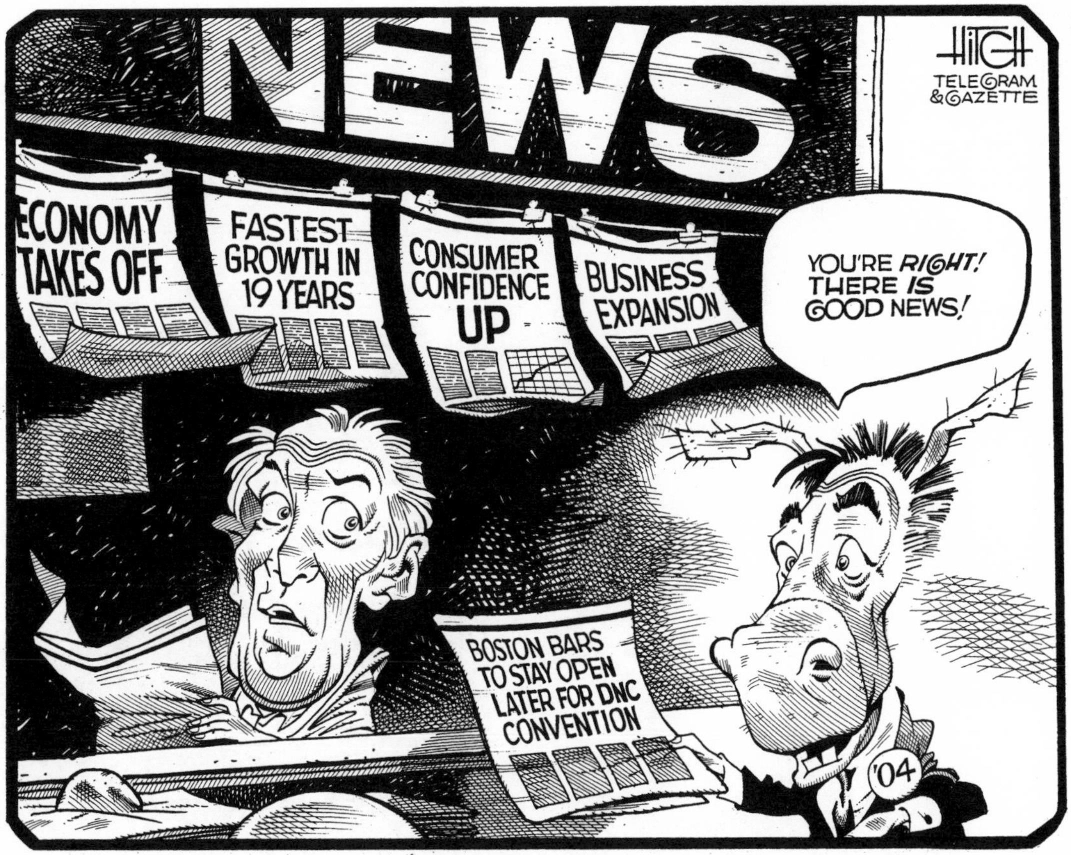

NEWS
HITCH TELEGRAM & GAZETTE
ECONOMY TAKES OFF
FASTEST GROWTH IN 19 YEARS
CONSUMER CONFIDENCE UP
BUSINESS EXPANSION
YOU'RE RIGHT! THERE IS GOOD NEWS!
BOSTON BARS TO STAY OPEN LATER FOR DNC CONVENTION
'04

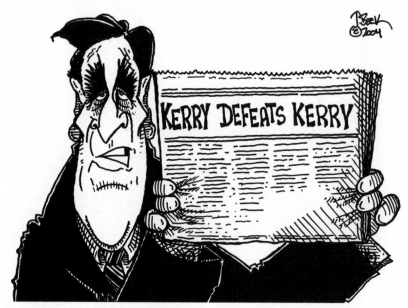

ROB SMITH, JR.
Courtesy DBR Media

TOM BECK
Courtesy Freeport Journal-Standard (Ill.)

LARRY WRIGHT
Courtesy Detroit News

SCOTT STANTIS
Courtesy Birmingham News

DICK LOCHER
Courtesy Chicago Tribune

JEFF DANZIGER
Courtesy Los Angeles Times Syndicate

SVEN VAN ASSCHE
Courtesy Hesam Acorn Publications

WALT HANDELSMAN
Courtesy Newsday

BARBARA BRANDON-CROFT
Courtesy Universal Press Syndicate

DICK LOCHER
Courtesy Chicago Tribune

LEADERSHIP THAT HAS UNITED THE REPUBLICAN PARTY

DAN DARROW
Courtesy The Giant Cabbage

REPUBLICAN TRINITY

Al Gorem
MASTER BETRAYED US! MY PRECIOUSSS! HE STOLE THE ELECTION FROM US! THEN HE TRICKED US INTO WAR! STUPID HOBBITSES SHOULD RESIGN!

GARY VARVEL
Courtesy Indianapolis Star

J. D. CROWE
Courtesy Mobile Register

THE OL' GIRL STILL GIVES A LOTTA MILK
VIETNAM
POLITICS

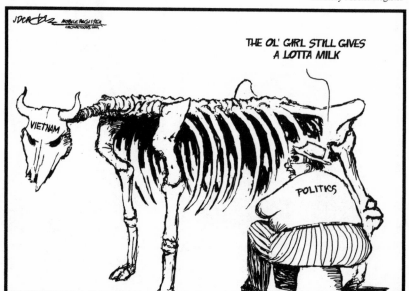

BILL GARNER
Courtesy Washington Times

JAKE FULLER
Courtesy Gainesville Sun

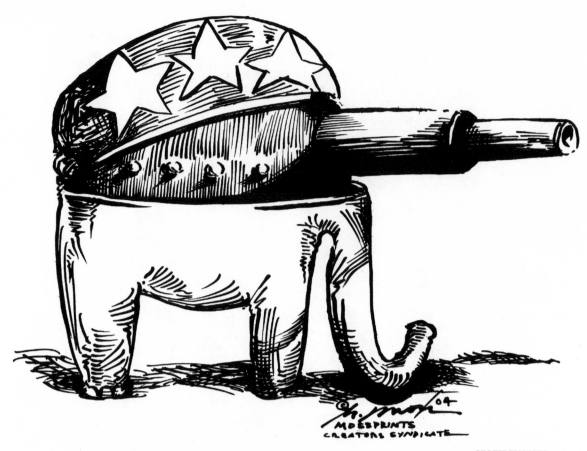

GEOFFREY MOSS
Courtesy Creators Syndicate

MARK STREETER
Courtesy Savannah Morning News

Foreign Affairs

More than 200 people, most of them children, were killed when Chechen terrorists stormed a school in Beslan in southern Russia. U.S. troops were sent to Haiti to restore order after rebels ousted President Jean-Bertrand Aristide, and the death toll in the civil war in Sudan rose during the year to an estimated two million.

Yasser Arafat, chairman of the Palestine Liberation Organization and considered by many to be the major obstacle to peace in the Middle East, died in Paris at age 75. The world was left to speculate about how the changing of the guard might affect the ongoing peace process.

Hamid Karzai, interim president of Afghanistan, was elected with 55 percent of the vote in that country's first-ever democratic election. Australian Premier John Howard, a staunch ally of America in the war in Iraq, was reelected in a landslide. His opponent had pledged to withdraw Australian troops from Iraq.

To quell rioting in Ivory Coast, French troops killed 27 and wounded 200 lawbreakers. France declined to seek United Nations approval in advance of the action.

The weak American dollar tended to boost the sale of American goods abroad during the year at the expense of European products.

MALCOLM MAYES
Courtesy Edmonton Journal

GUY BADEAUX
Courtesy LeDroit

GRAEME MacKAY
Courtesy Hamilton Spectator

STEVE BREEN
Courtesy San Diego Union-Tribune

GARY MARKSTEIN
Courtesy Milwaukee Journal Sentinel

JOSEPH F. O'MAHONEY
Courtesy The Patriot Ledger

JIM HUNT
Courtesy Charlotte Post

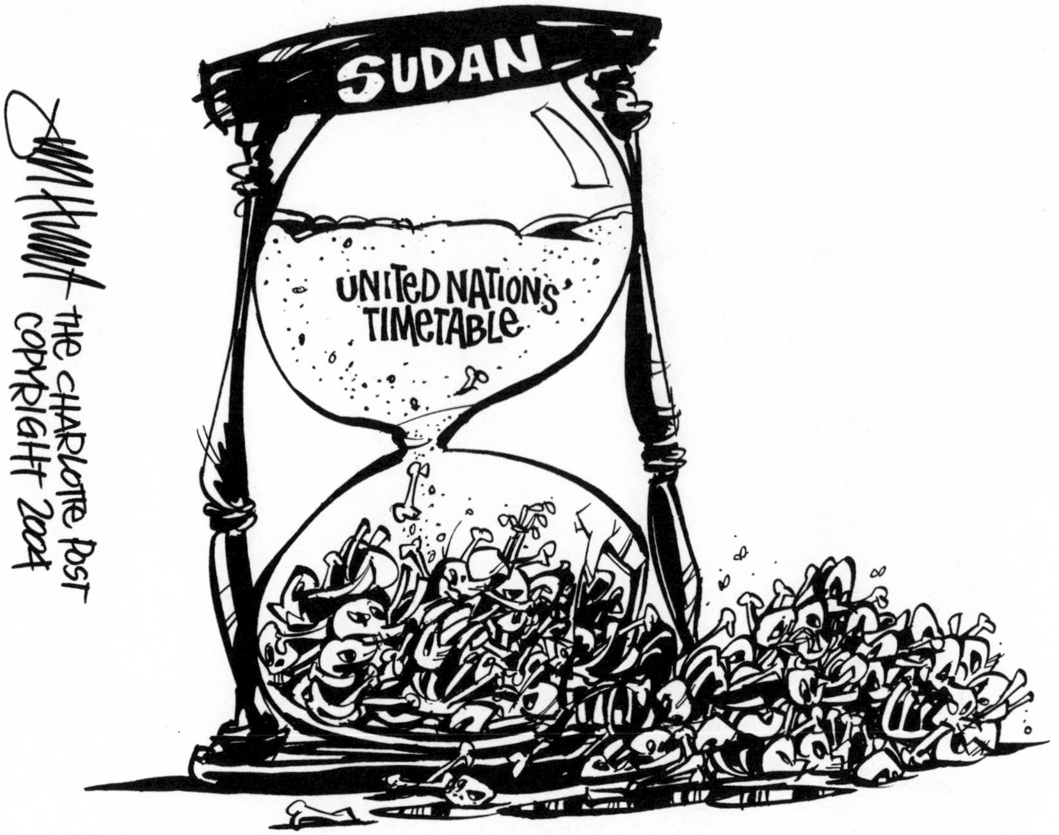
SUDAN
UNITED NATIONS' TIMETABLE
JIM HUNT - THE CHARLOTTE POST COPYRIGHT 2004

DAN CARINO
Courtesy Knight Ridder Services

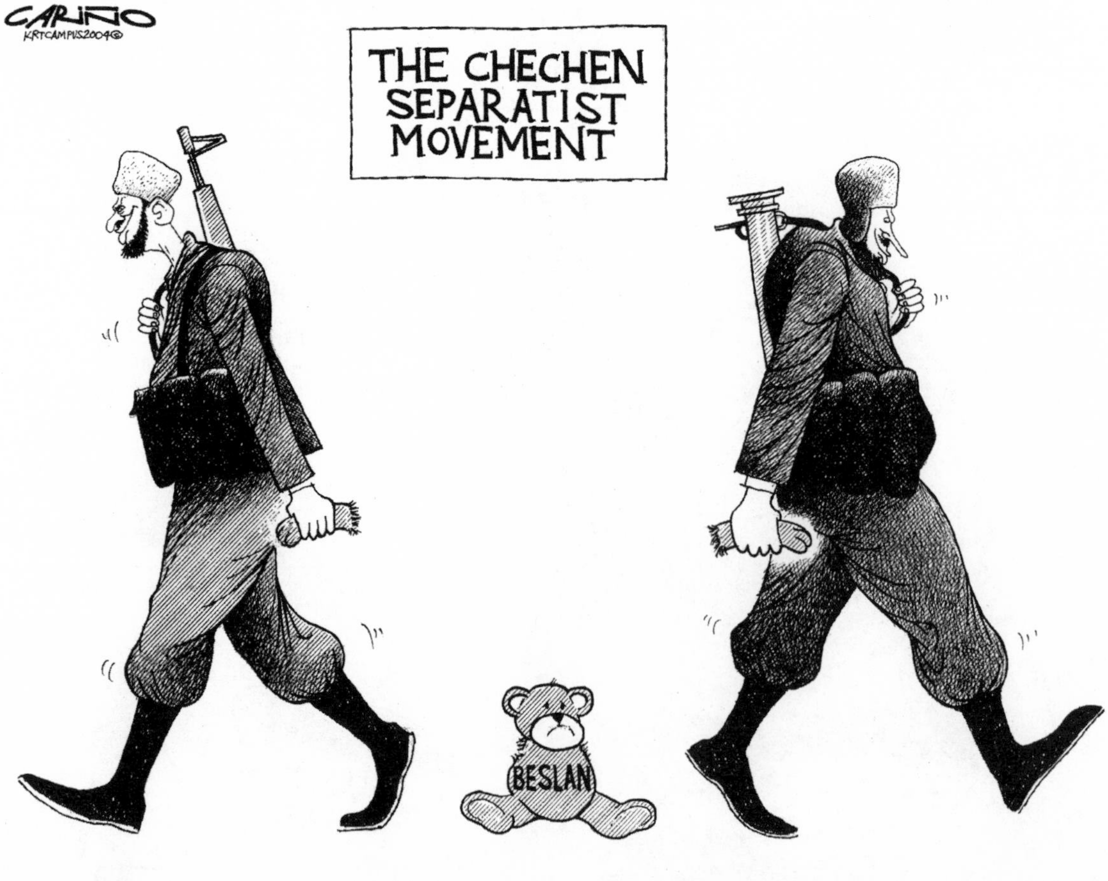
CARINO
KRTCAMPUS2004©
THE CHECHEN SEPARATIST MOVEMENT
BESLAN

MARK THORNHILL
Courtesy North County Times

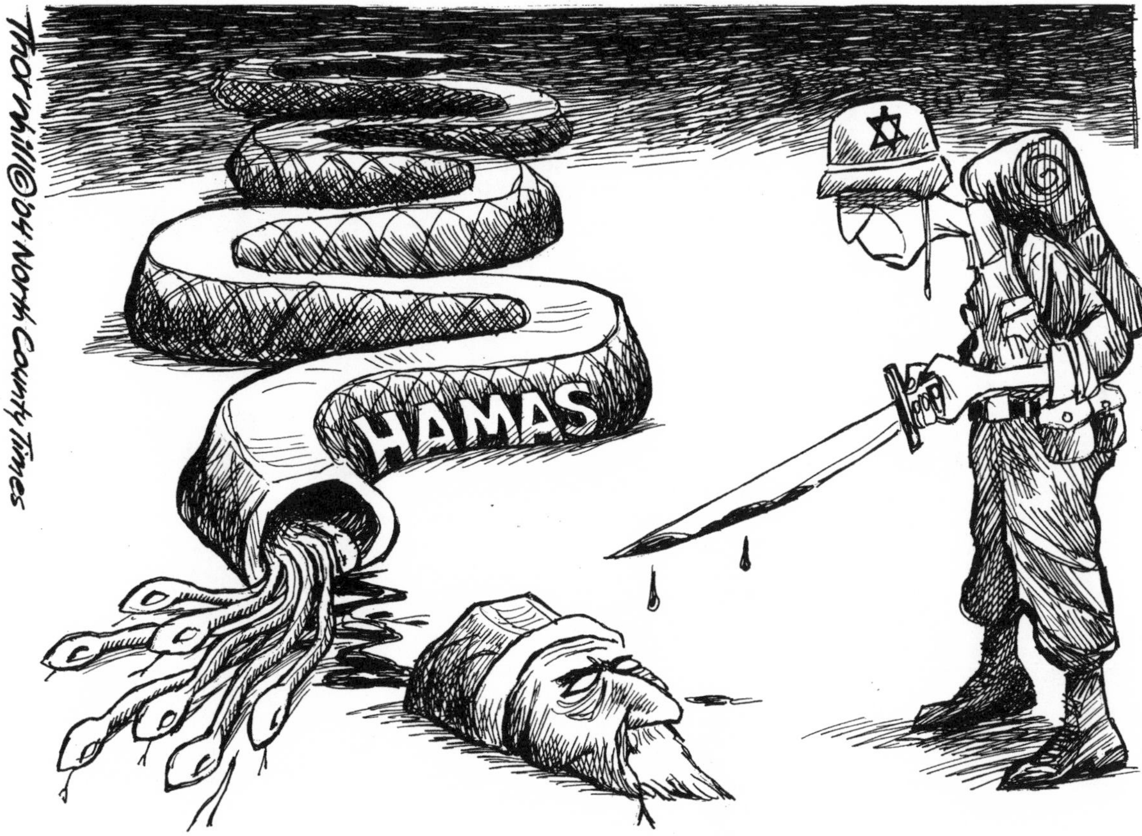
Thornhill©04 North County Times
HAMAS

MICHAEL RAMIREZ
Courtesy Los Angeles Times

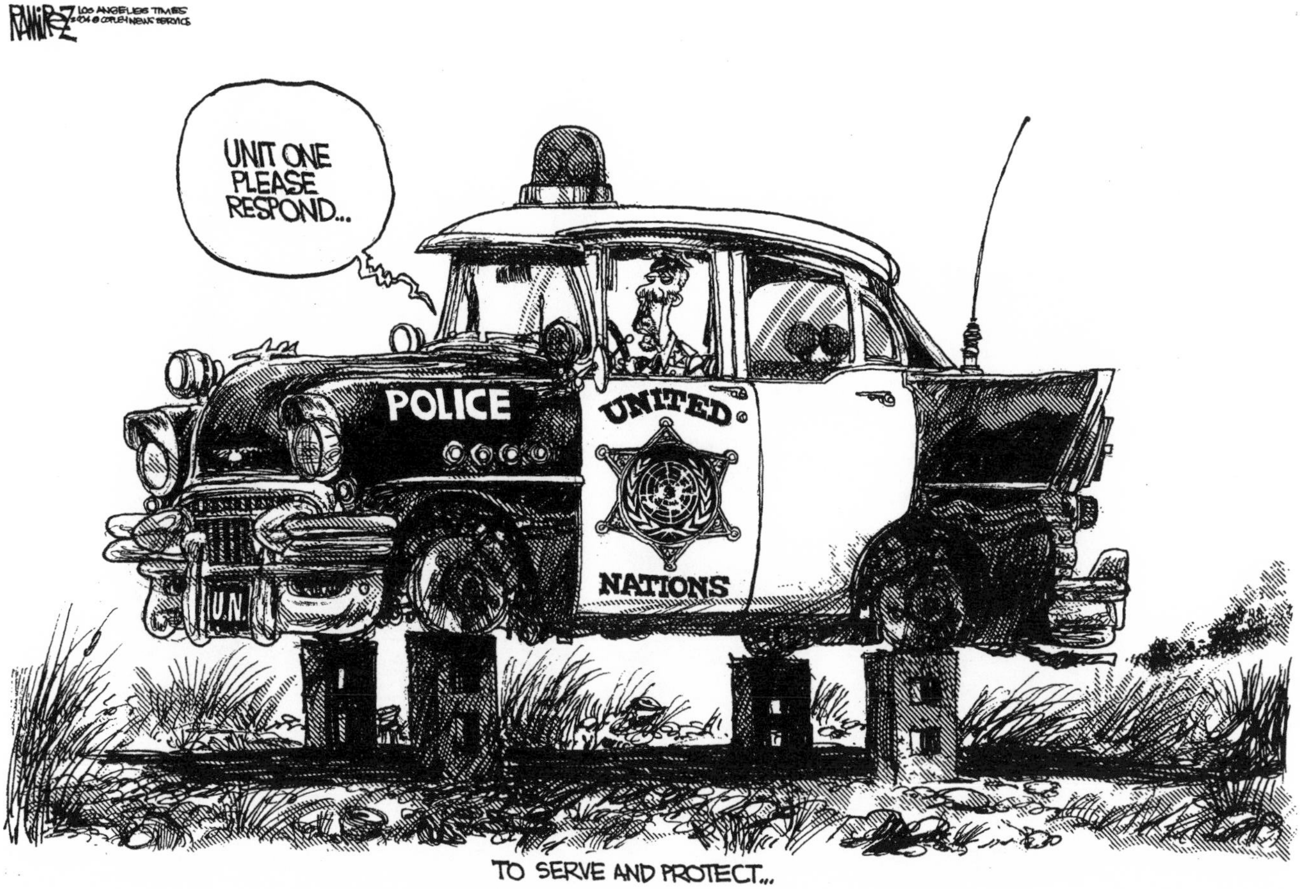
RAMIREZ
UNIT ONE PLEASE RESPOND...
POLICE
UNITED
NATIONS
U.N

TO SERVE AND PROTECT...

RANAN LURIE
Courtesy Cartoonews International Syndicate

"Why do you keep smiling when your Dollar's falling?"

THE ARAB WORLD'S REACTION TO NICK BERG'S MURDER.....

DAN CARINO
Courtesy Knight Ridder Services

ED FISCHER
Courtesy Rochester Post-Bulletin

JUSTIN DeFREITAS
Courtesy Berkeley Daily Planet

THE STATE OF PALESTINE

JACK HIGGINS
Courtesy Chicago Sun-Times

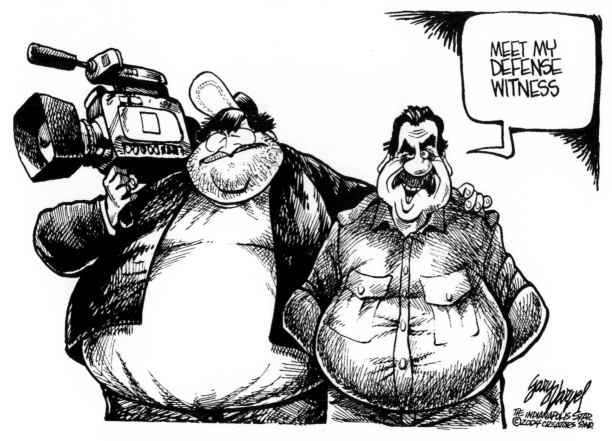

GARY VARVEL
Courtesy Indianapolis Star

DAVID HITCH
Courtesy Worcester Telegram and Gazette

Media / Entertainment

CBS and anchorman Dan Rather were caught up in an embarrassing incident with the airing of charges that President Bush refused to report as ordered while he was a member of the Texas National Guard. Rather vigorously defended the story until it became obvious that it was false. Rather later announced he was resigning from his anchorman duties to do other things.

In 1976, polls showed that 7 out of 10 Americans had confidence in the press. Today, some 53 percent report that they do not trust the media to tell the truth. Viewers of the 2004 Super Bowl were startled when "a wardrobe malfunction" exposed the breast of a performer.

Mel Gibson's movie *The Passion of Christ* played to record audiences despite unrelenting opposition from liberals, and activist Michael Moore released his *Fahrenheit 9/11,* which pummeled Bush and his policies. Oprah Winfrey celebrated her 19th season on television with a huge automobile giveaway, and bestselling author Kitty Kelley published a biting portrait of the Bush dynasty.

Most media in Europe supported John Kerry in the presidential campaign and seemed baffled by support among voters for Bush. Kerry also enjoyed the support of Hollywood, where the Walt Disney Entertainment Group restructured its leadership after a major revolt by shareholders.

JOHN DEERING
Courtesy Arkansas Democrat-Gazette

PAUL NOWAK
Courtesy Scripps-Howard Newspapers

ERIC SMITH
Courtesy Annapolis Capital-Gazette

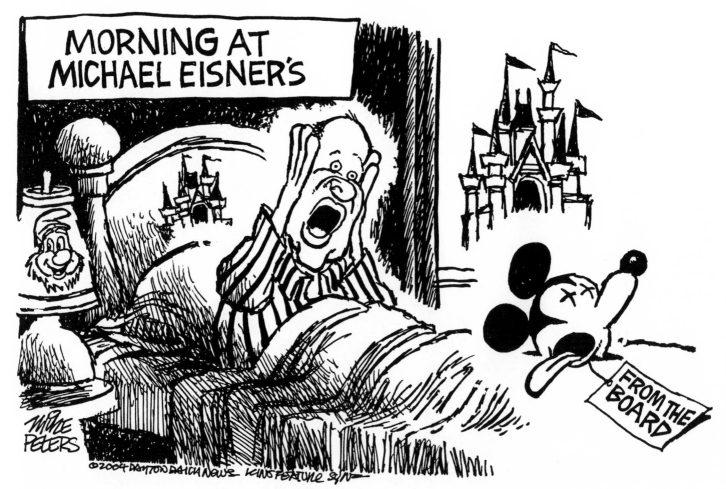

MIKE PETERS
Courtesy Dayton Daily News

JERRY BARNETT
Courtesy Indianapolis Star

ROBERT ARIAIL
Courtesy The State (S.C.)

TERRY WISE
Courtesy Ratland.com

CHARLIE HALL
Courtesy Rhode Island News Group

"I'm sorry but your car loan was declined. However we CAN offer you 2 tickets to a taping of OPRAH...."

CHUCK ASAY
Courtesy Colorado Springs Gazette-Telegraph

WAYNE STROOT
Courtesy Hastings Tribune

COLIN HAYES
Courtesy Rightoons.com

JOE HOFFECKER
Courtesy American City Business Journals

STEVE LINDSTROM
Courtesy Duluth News-Tribune

106

DAVE SATTLER
Courtesy Lafayette Journal and Courier

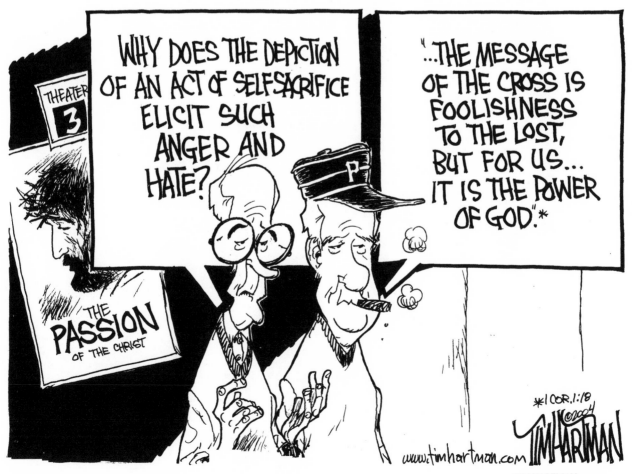

TIM HARTMAN
Courtesy Beaver County Times

107

GUY BADEAUX
Courtesy LeDroit

MICHAEL MOORE RETURNS FROM CANNES

JIM LANGE
Courtesy Daily Oklahoman

BARBARA BRANDON-CROFT
Courtesy Universal Press Syndicate

LARRY WRIGHT
Courtesy Detroit News

JACK HIGGINS
Courtesy Chicago Sun-Times

109

WAYNE STAYSKAL
Courtesy Tribune Media Services

JEFF PARKER
Courtesy Florida Today

The Economy

The economy continued to rebound during the year, albeit slowly, and stocks remained strong. Consumer attitudes about future prospects brightened, and job markets produced more openings, particularly in high-tech fields. Outsourcing of jobs slowed somewhat during the year.

All of the world's major economies, including the United States, have lost jobs in manufacturing. In the U.S., they are down 11 percent, while Japan and China have lost 15 percent and Brazil 20 percent.

Even with some help from the Bush Administration and Congress, prescription drug prices remained at a high level. Furthermore, all medical costs continued to outpace the rate of inflation, which remained low.

Pump prices for gasoline shot through the roof as crude oil prices topped $53 a barrel. The oil price increase was caused partly by greater demand from countries such as China, Indonesia, and India, which are becoming more affluent. Adding to the problem was uncertainty over Saudi Arabia and Iraq. Clearly, the prospects for moderate gasoline prices do not seem bright. For the U.S., the major downside is a whopping trade deficit that has hit $413 billion, the highest since World War II.

CHARLES DANIEL
Courtesy Knoxville News-Sentinel

111

STEVEN TEMPLETON
Courtesy Observer-Times

GEORGE DANBY
Courtesy Bangor Daily News

BILL WHITEHEAD
Courtesy Kansas City Business Journal

ED COLLEY
Courtesy Boston Globe South/Northwest

Labor Day 2004

JOHN SPENCER
Courtesy Philadelphia Business Journal

ED GAMBLE
Courtesy Florida Times-Union

STEVE KELLEY
Courtesy The Times-Picayune

BILL WHITEHEAD
Courtesy Kansas City Business Journal

114

MIKE SCOTT
Courtesy Newark Star-Ledger

STAN BURDICK
Courtesy Lake Champlain Weekly

BOB UNELL
Courtesy Kansas City Star

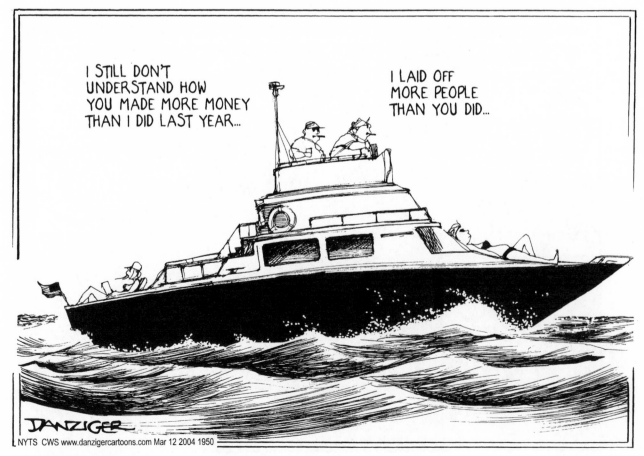

JEFF DANZIGER
Courtesy Los Angeles Times Syndicate

STEVE McBRIDE
Courtesy Independence Daily Reporter

KARL WIMER
Courtesy Denver Business Journal

DANIEL FENECH
Courtesy Saline Reporter

ED FISCHER
Courtesy Rochester Post-Bulletin

RUSSELL HODIN
Courtesy The New Times

ALAN VITELLO
Courtesy Greeley Tribune

WILLIAM FLINT
Courtesy Dallas Morning News

119

DIRECT DEPOSIT

JIM DYKE
Courtesy Jefferson City News-Tribune

POL GALVEZ
Courtesy Philippine News

TIM JACKSON
Courtesy Chicago Defender

CLAY JONES
Courtesy Free Lance-Star (Va.)

G. MARTY STEIN
Courtesy LaPrensa

121

MATT DAVIES
Courtesy The Journal News (N.Y.)

CHUCK LEGGE
Courtesy The Frontiersman

JESSE SPRINGER
Courtesy Springercreative.com

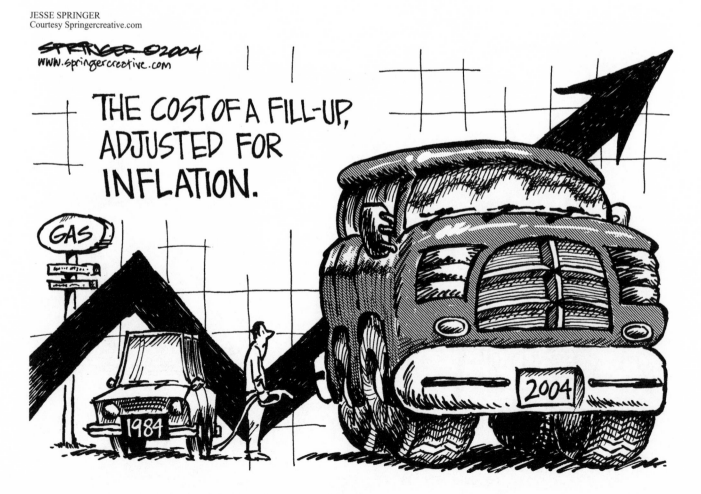

CLAY BENNETT
Courtesy Christian Science Monitor

WILLIAM FLINT
Courtesy Dallas Morning News

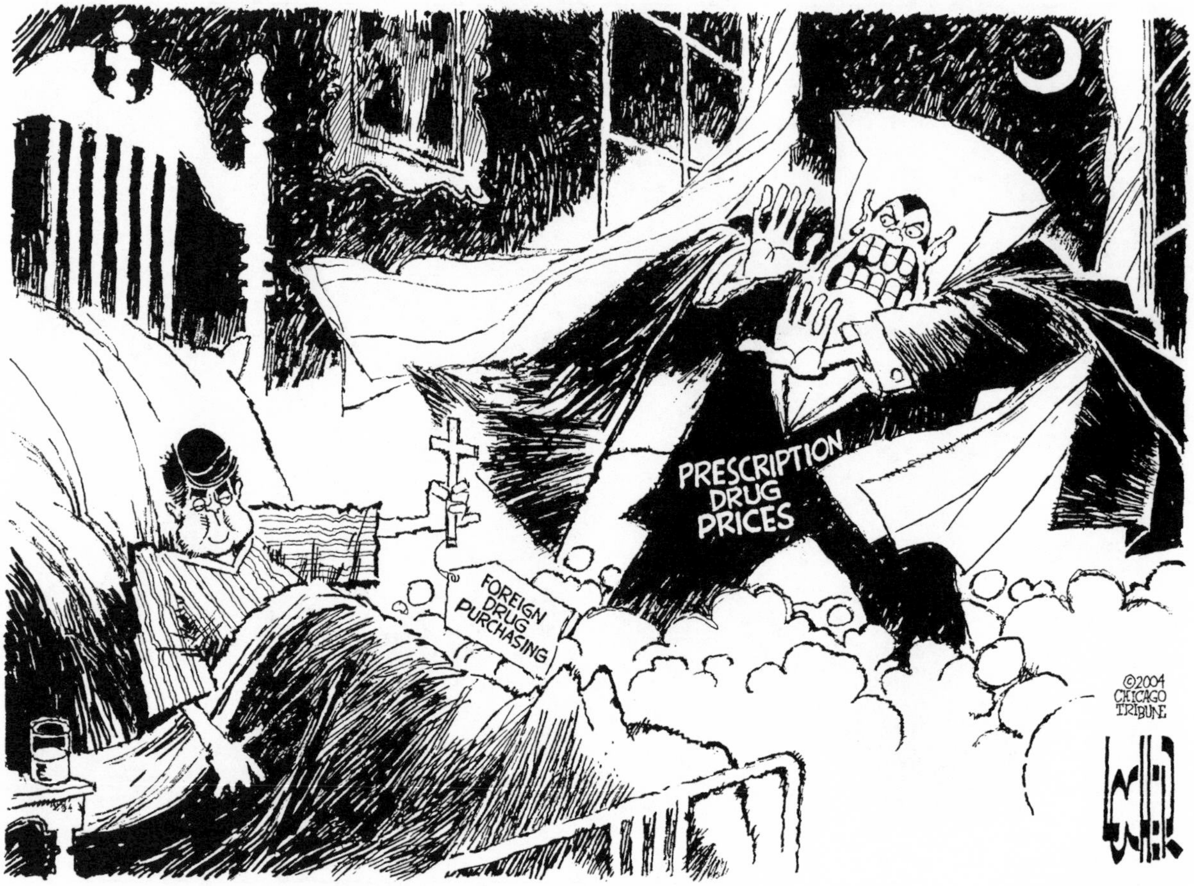
PRESCRIPTION
DRUG
PRICES
FOREIGN
DRUG
PURCHASING
©2004
CHICAGO
TRIBUNE
LOCHER

DICK LOCHER
Courtesy Chicago Tribune

MIKE KEEFE
Courtesy Denver Post

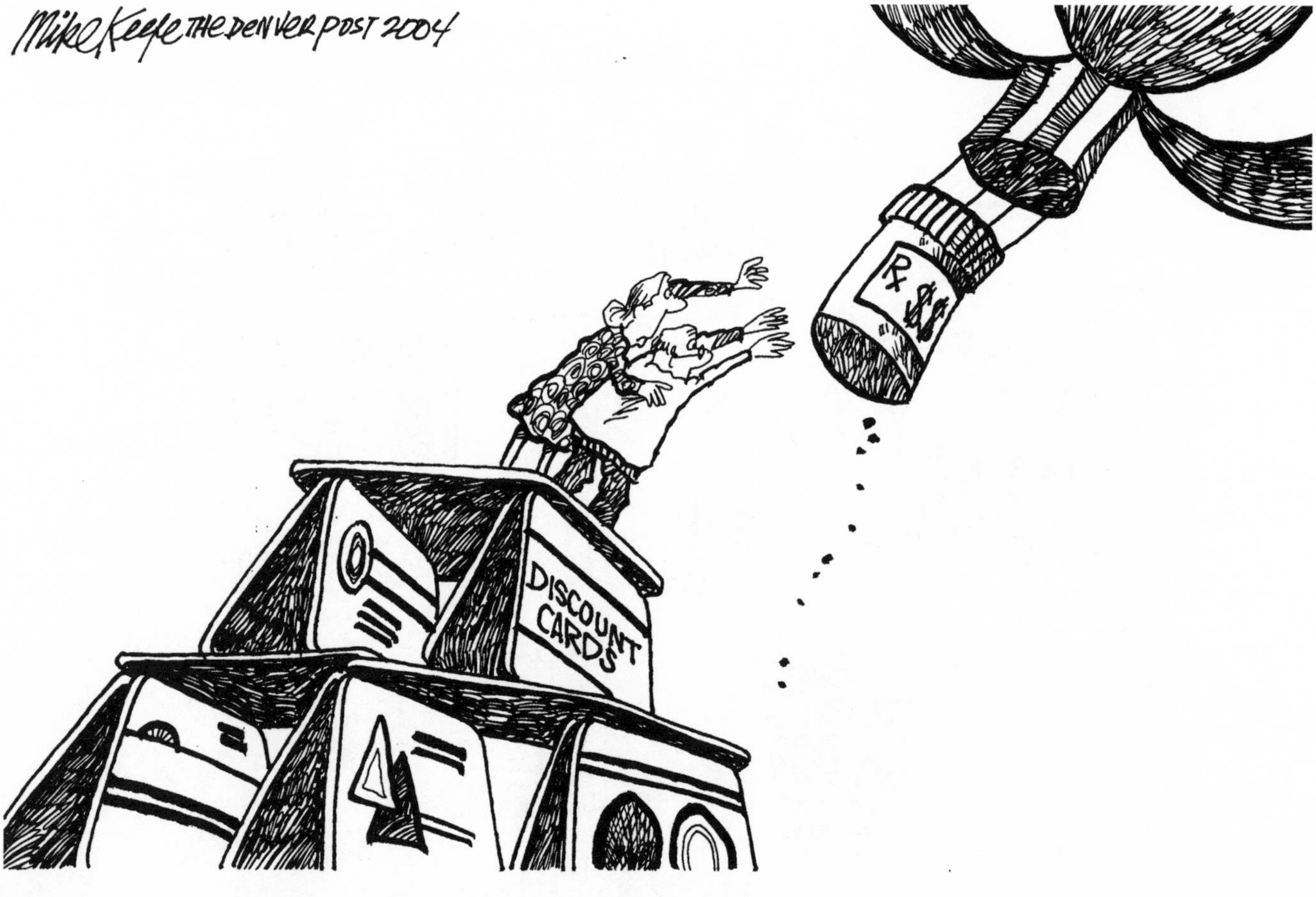
Mike Keefe THE DENVER POST 2004
DISCOUNT
CARDS
Rx
$$

Health / Environment

Florida was ravaged by a tropical storm and four hurricanes within a six-week span, causing an estimated $30 billion in damage. Some two million homes and businesses were left without power, some for weeks. In the West and Alaska, almost 3.5 million acres of forests burned amid a continuing drought. Mount St. Helens sent a thick, gray cloud thousands of feet into the air on October 5, but the major eruption feared by scientists did not occur.

America remains divided on the matter of stem-cell research. A shortage of flu shots late in the year caused a run on clinics and hospitals throughout the U.S. The severe shortage was made public when British regulators cited contamination problems for closing one of the two companies that manufacture vaccine for the U.S. market.

A recent study of fifteen nations found that American children were the fattest, with the rate of obesity more than double that of twenty years ago. Declining physical activity and a huge increase in the consumption of fast food and soft drinks were blamed.

One case of mad cow disease was reported in the U.S. in late 2003, causing U.S.-produced beef to be banned by several countries for a time.

CHRIS BRITT
Courtesy State Journal-Register

TOM BECK
Courtesy Freeport Journal-Standard (Ill.)

DAVE SATTLER
Courtesy Lafayette Journal and Courier

JESSE SPRINGER
Courtesy Springercreative.com

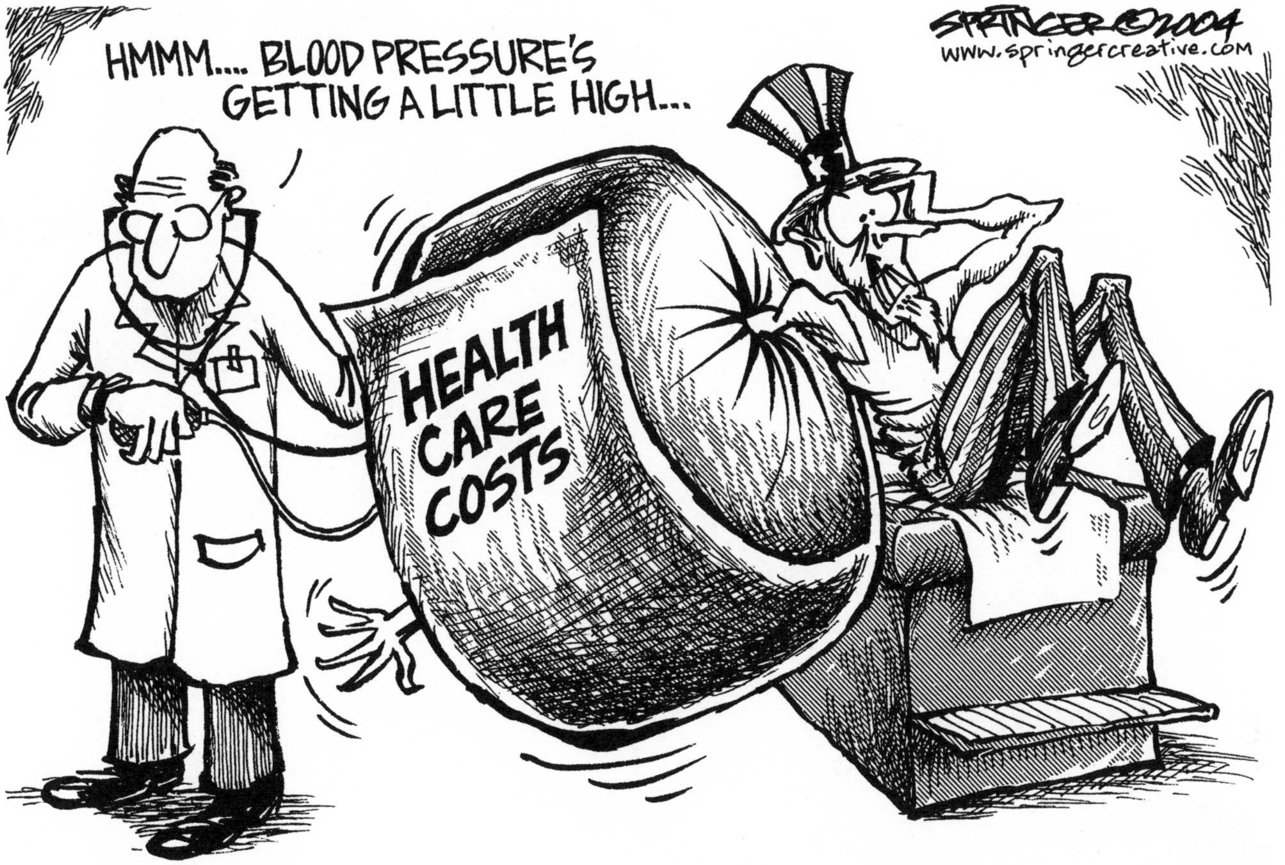
SPRINGER ©2004
www.springercreative.com
HMMM.... BLOOD PRESSURE'S GETTING A LITTLE HIGH...
HEALTH CARE COSTS

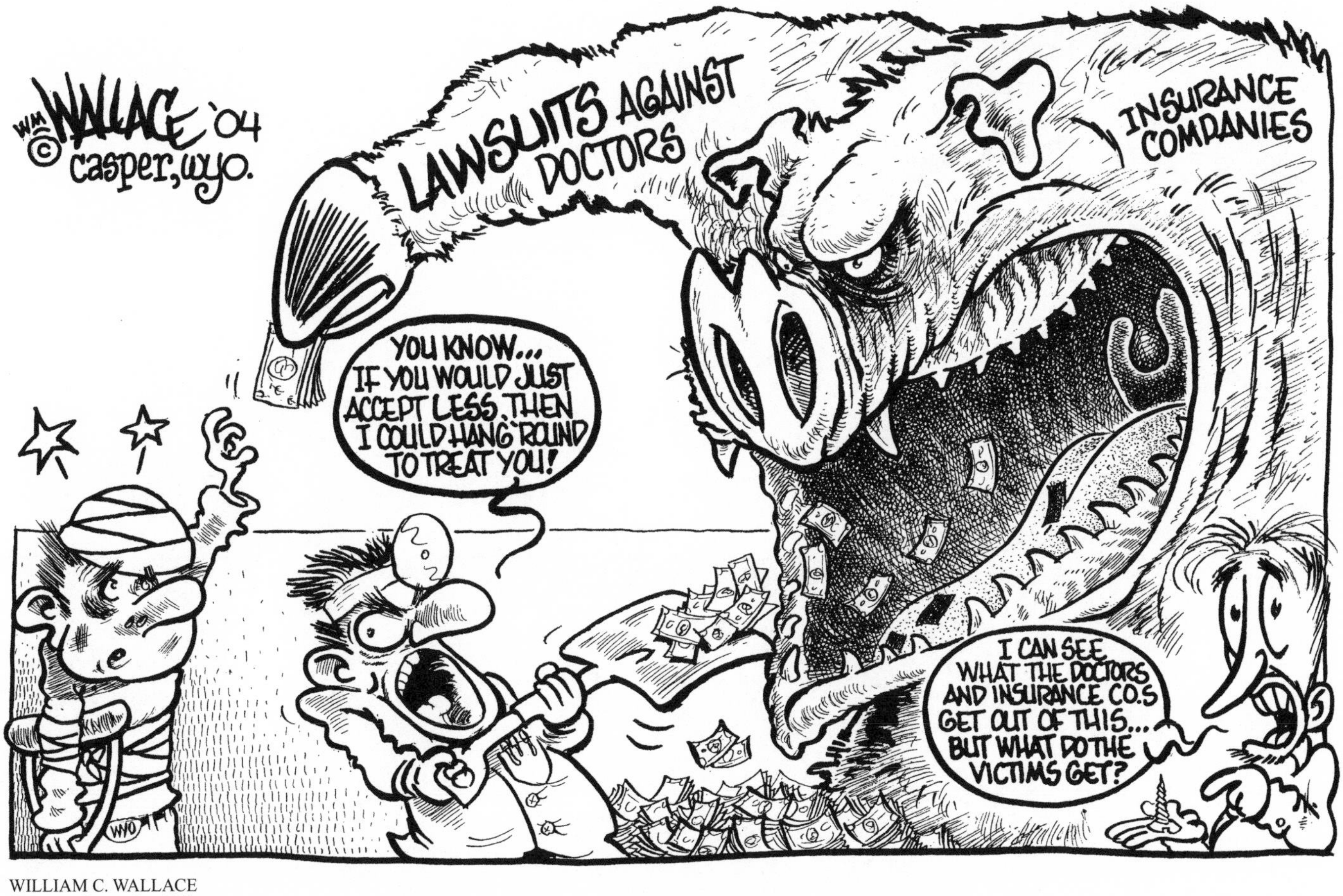
WM WALLACE '04 © casper, wyo.
LAWSUITS AGAINST DOCTORS
INSURANCE COMPANIES
YOU KNOW... IF YOU WOULD JUST ACCEPT LESS, THEN I COULD HANG 'ROUND TO TREAT YOU!
I CAN SEE WHAT THE DOCTORS AND INSURANCE CO.S GET OUT OF THIS... BUT WHAT DO THE VICTIMS GET?

WILLIAM C. WALLACE
Courtesy Casper Star-Tribune

TIM BENSON
Courtesy Argus-Leader (S.D.)

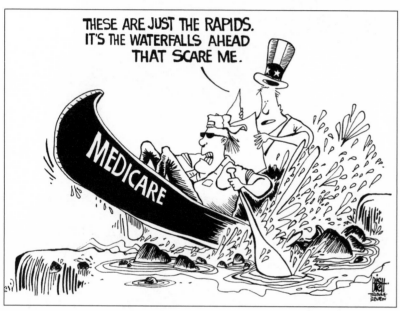

RANDY BISH
Courtesy Tribune-Review (Pa.)

DANA SUMMERS
Courtesy Orlando Sentinel

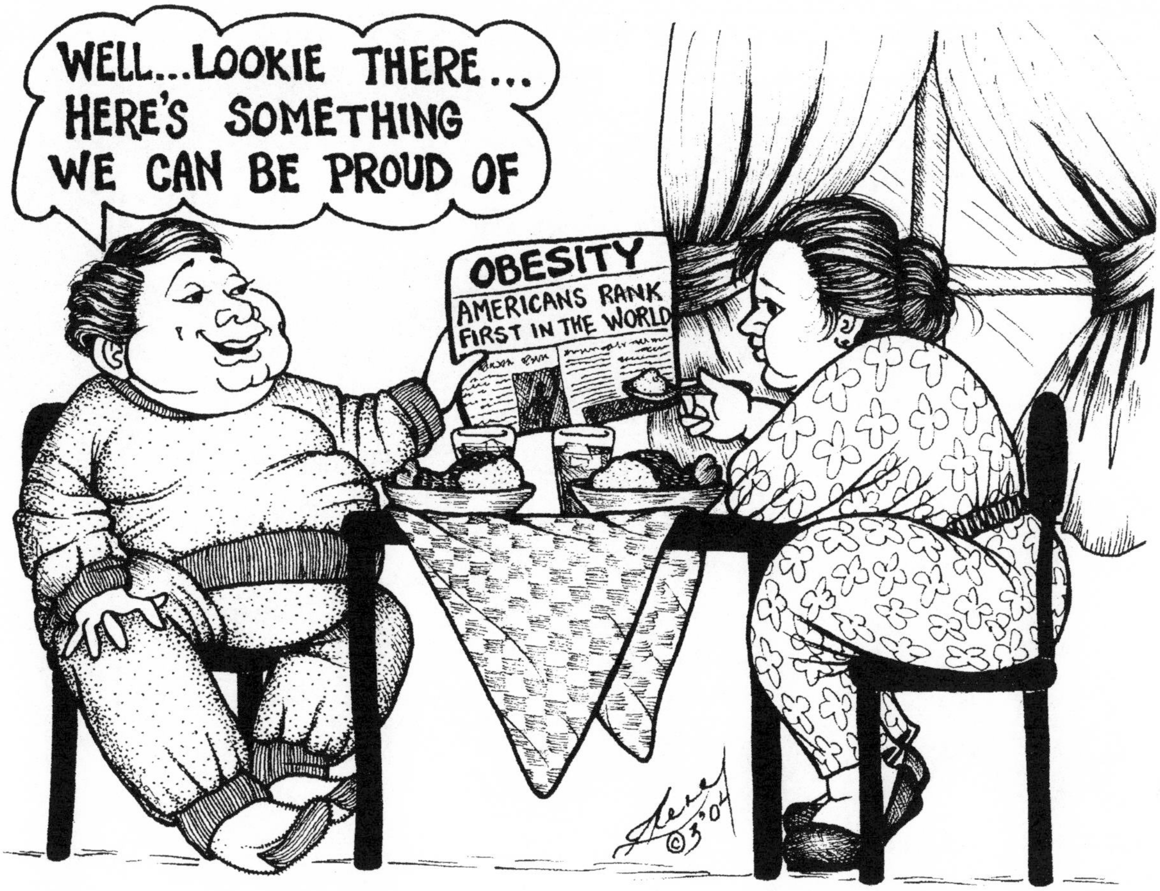
WELL...LOOKIE THERE... HERE'S SOMETHING WE CAN BE PROUD OF
OBESITY
AMERICANS RANK FIRST IN THE WORLD

IRENE JOSLIN
Courtesy Brown County Democrat

JIMMY MARGULIES
Courtesy The Record (N.J.)

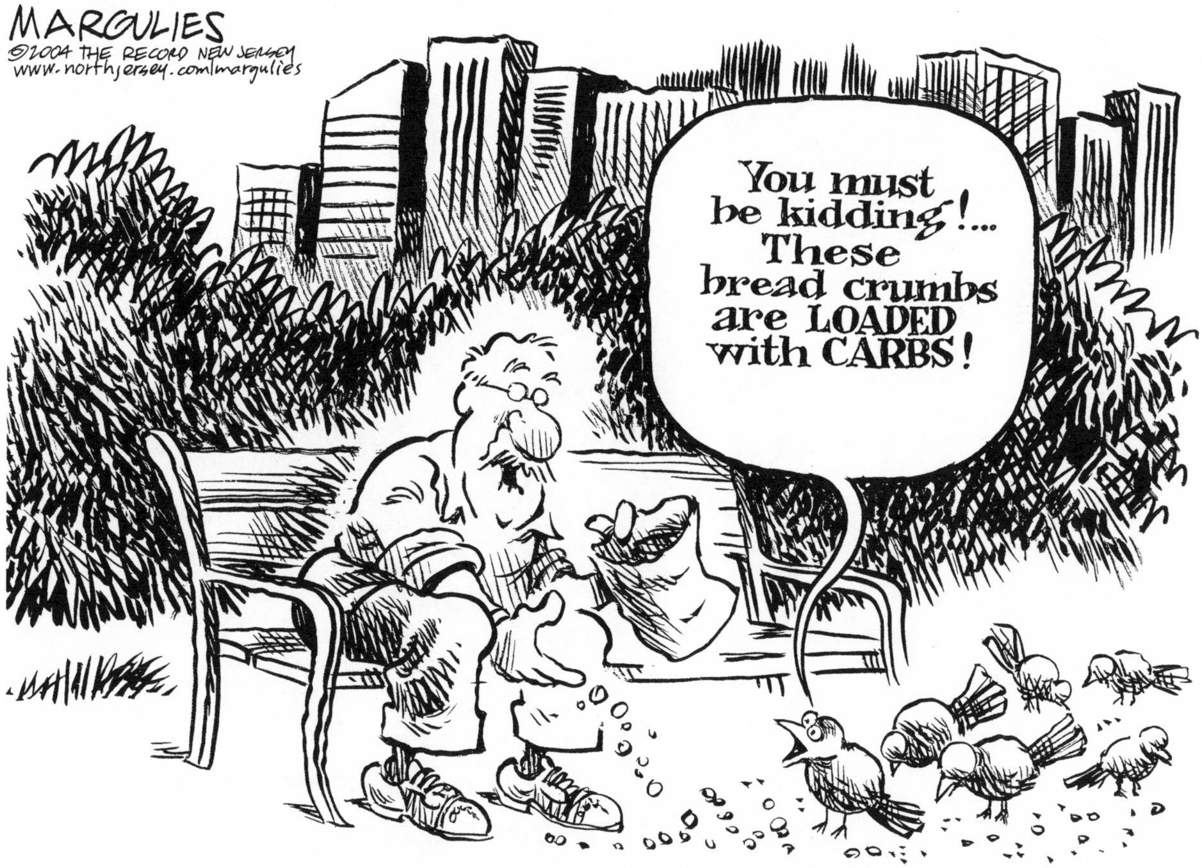
MARGULIES
©2004 THE RECORD NEW JERSEY
www.northjersey.com/margulies
You must be kidding!... These bread crumbs are LOADED with CARBS!

LARRY WRIGHT
Courtesy Detroit News

JEFF PARKER
Courtesy Florida Today

RACING TO AN EARLY FINISH...

BRUCE PLANTE
Courtesy Chattanooga Times

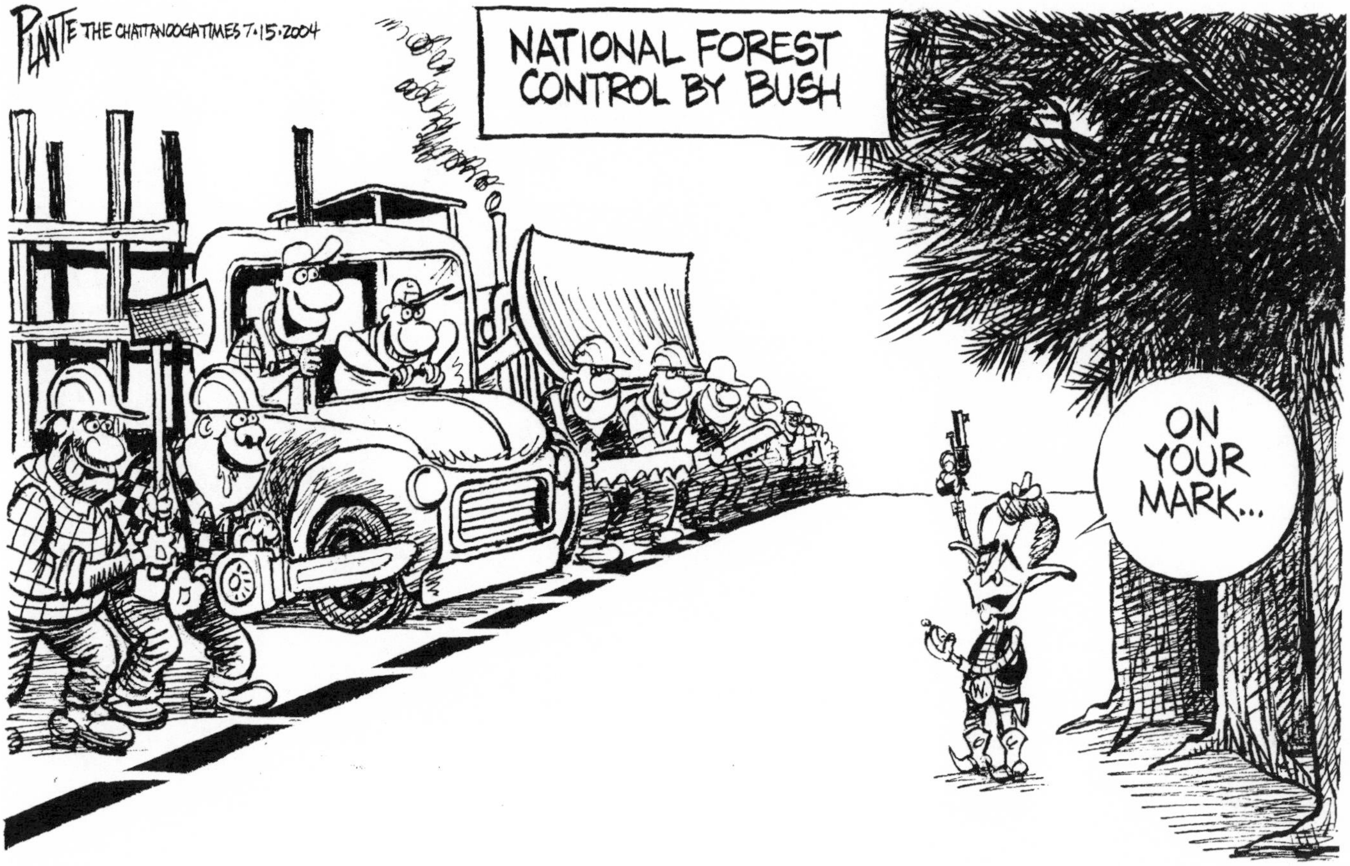
PLANTE THE CHATTANOOGA TIMES 7•15•2004
NATIONAL FOREST CONTROL BY BUSH
ON YOUR MARK...

STEVE GREENBERG
Courtesy Ventura County Star

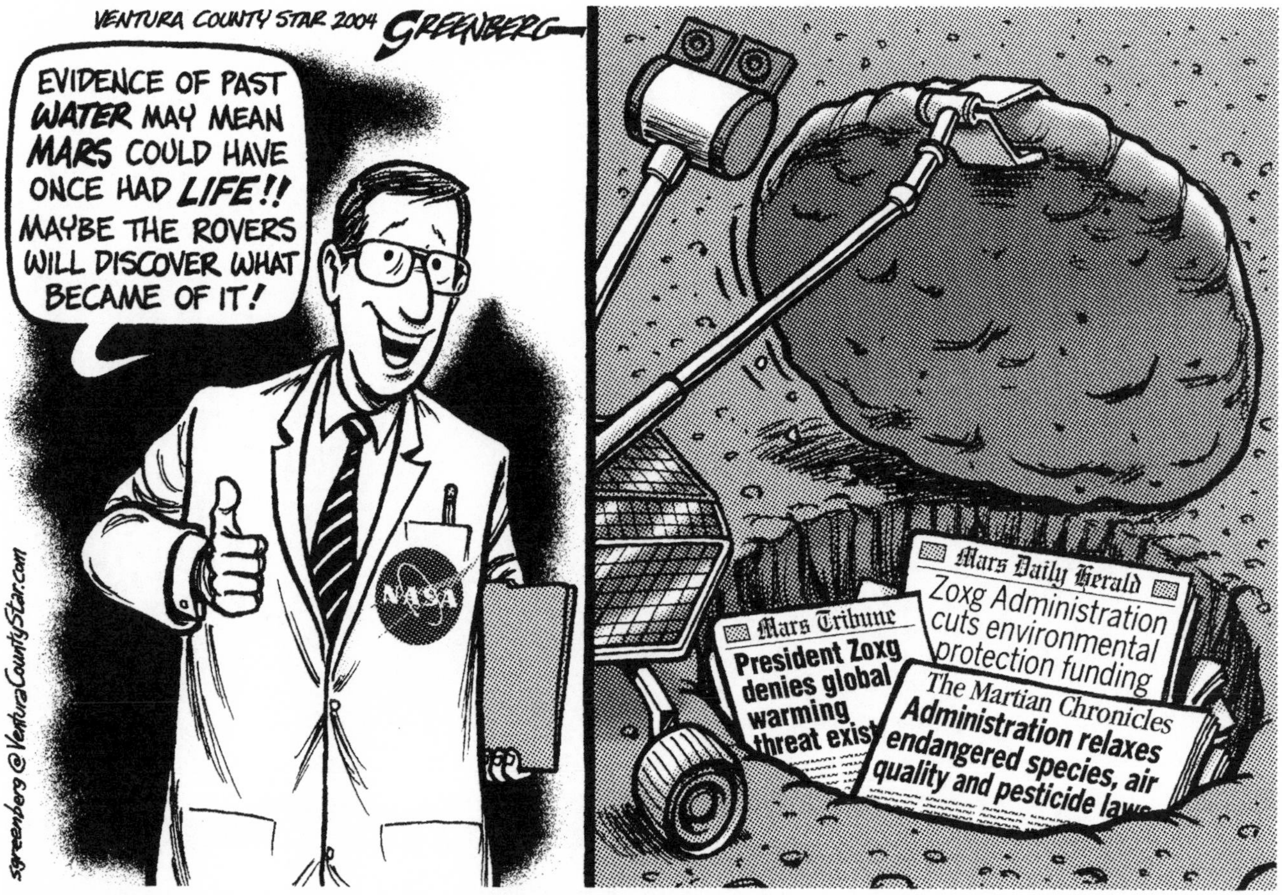
VENTURA COUNTY STAR 2004 GREENBERG
EVIDENCE OF PAST WATER MAY MEAN MARS COULD HAVE ONCE HAD LIFE!! MAYBE THE ROVERS WILL DISCOVER WHAT BECAME OF IT!
NASA
sgreenberg@VenturaCountyStar.com
Mars Daily Herald
Zoxg Administration cuts environmental protection funding
Mars Tribune
President Zoxg denies global warming threat exist
The Martian Chronicles
Administration relaxes endangered species, air quality and pesticide laws

ED HALL
Courtesy Baker County Press

ED FISCHER
Courtesy Rochester Post-Bulletin

RICK McKEE
Courtesy Augusta Chronicle

IF T.V. REPORTERS COVERED FOREST FIRES LIKE they COVER HURRICANES

PAUL FELL
Courtesy Lincoln Journal Star

JAMES McCLOSKEY
Courtesy The Daily News Leader (Va.)

RICHARD CROWSON
Courtesy Witchita Eagle

JOHN AUCTER
Courtesy Grand Rapids Business Journal

JIMMY MARGULIES
Courtesy The Record (N.J.)

JOE MAJESKI
Courtesy The Times-Leader (Pa.)

J. D. CROWE
Courtesy Mobile Register

DOUG MacGREGOR
Courtesy Fort Myers News-Press

ROB HARRIMAN
Courtesy Portland Tribune

JIM HUNT
Courtesy Charlotte Post

DOUG MacGREGOR
Courtesy Fort Myers News-Press

TERRY WISE
Courtesy Ratland.com

BOB WIEGERS
Courtesy Rockford Register-Star

ALAN J. NASH
Courtesy Gering Courier/North Platte Bulletin

DOUGLAS REGALIA
Courtesy Contra Costa Newspaper Group

PAUL FELL
Courtesy Lincoln Journal Star

The PRxISONER

PRICE GOUGING
USE ONLY AS DIRECTED

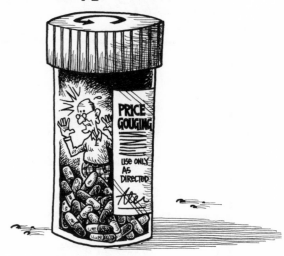

DENNIS DRAUGHON
Courtesy Scranton Times

YOUR NEW MEDICARE DRUG CARD:
JOKER
DRUG INDUSTRY
THIS CARD GOOD FOR 10% OFF OF THE 200% INFLATED PRICE OF YOUR PRESCRIPTION
$500 BILLION JUST DOESN'T GO AS FAR AS IT USED TO...
4-15
©2004 THE WICHITA EAGLE

RICHARD CROWSON
Courtesy Witchita Eagle

WHAT REGULATIONS?
TEXAS
WHAT OZONE?
EPA
WHAT HAK HAK HAK INCOMPETENCE

ETTA HULME
Courtesy Fort Worth Star-Telegram

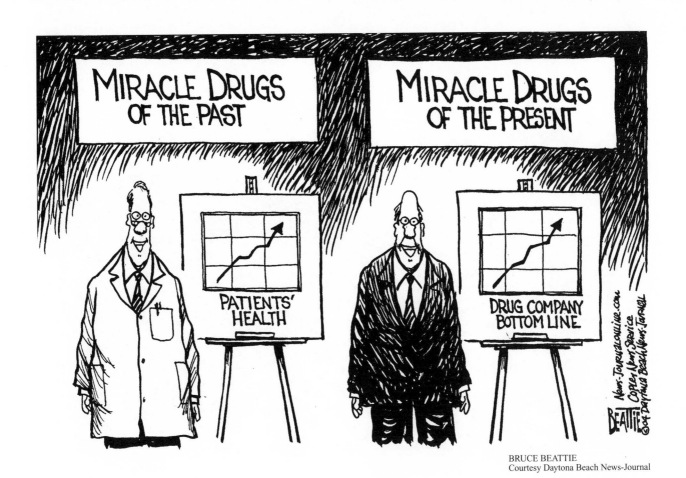

BRUCE BEATTIE
Courtesy Daytona Beach News-Journal

ED HALL
Courtesy Baker County Press

141

JEFF DANZIGER
Courtesy Los Angeles Times Syndicate

JOHN SHERFFIUS
Courtesy jsherffius@aol.com

Military Affairs

In late May, photographs were published showing American military police abusing and humiliating naked Arab prisoners at Abu Ghraib prison in Iraq. Military officials, it appeared, had failed to act on reports of abuses uncovered the previous year. The prison had virtually no trained professional correction officers and had major sanitation problems.

Hooded, naked detainees were held on leashes and forced to participate in humiliating sexual acts while their guards laughed and joked. The Army launched an investigation, and as more photographs were found, President Bush was moved to issue a personal apology. Seven soldiers were charged with prisoner abuse, and at year's end one had been convicted and given a sentence of eight years.

Pat Tillman, who gave up a lucrative career as a professional football player to become a soldier and fight terrorism, was killed in action in Afghanistan. He had walked away from a three-year, $3.6 million contract with the Arizona Cardinals of the National Football League to join the Army Rangers in 2002. He was killed in April, apparently by friendly fire.

ED GAMBLE
Courtesy Florida Times-Union

Independence Day!

STEVEN TEMPLETON
Courtesy Observer-Times

JOEL THORNHILL
Courtesy Lawrence County Record

STEVE LINDSTROM
Courtesy Duluth News-Tribune

REX BABIN
Courtesy Sacramento Bee

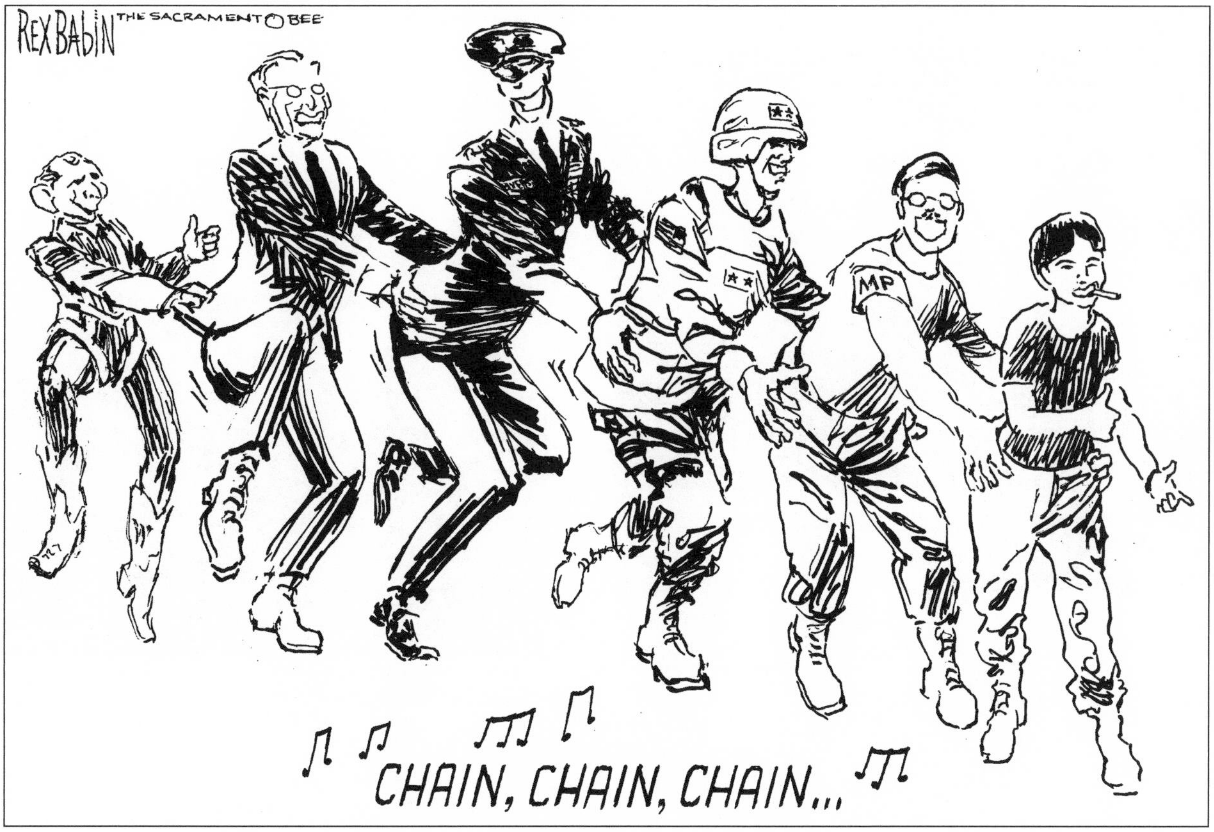
REX BABIN THE SACRAMENTO BEE
CHAIN, CHAIN, CHAIN...

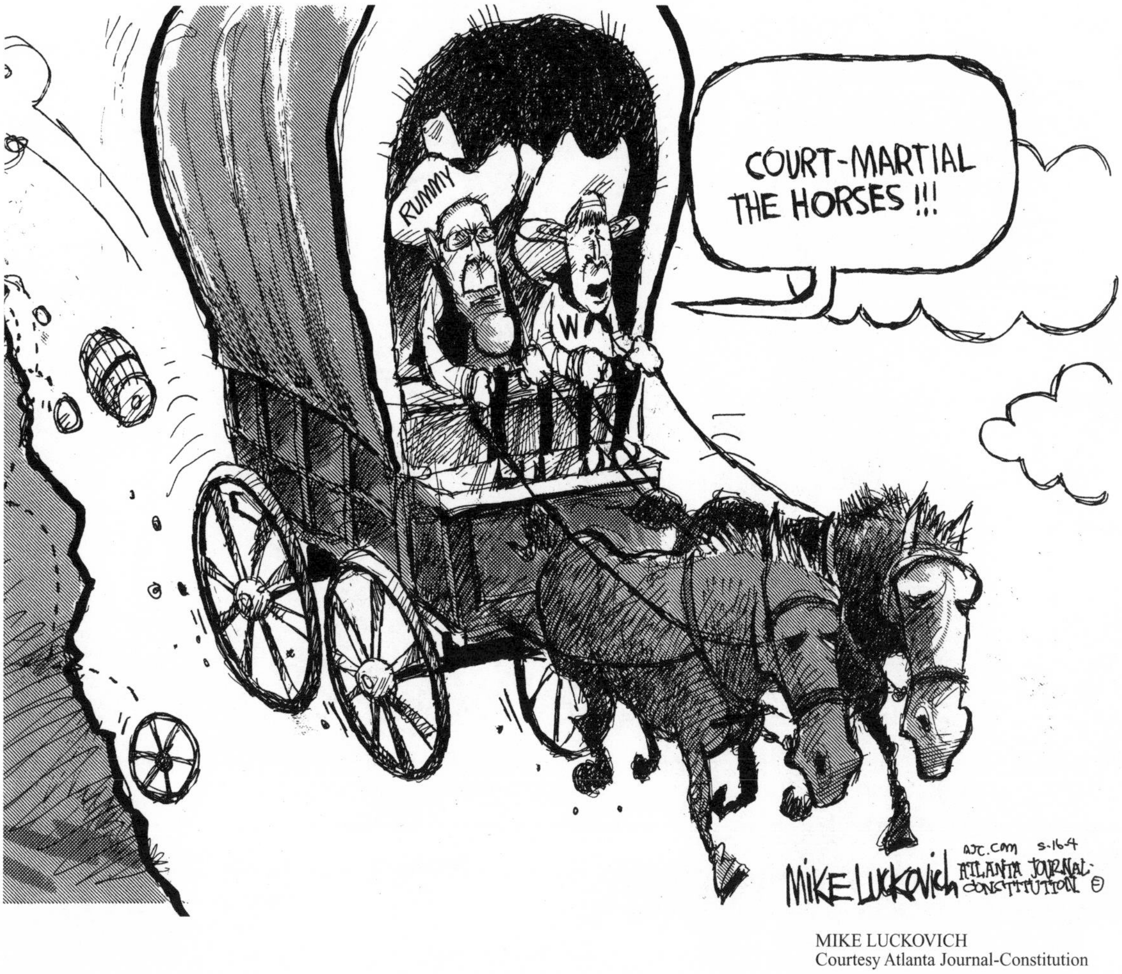
COURT-MARTIAL THE HORSES !!!
RUMMY
W
MIKE LUCKOVICH
AJC.COM 5-16-4
ATLANTA JOURNAL-CONSTITUTION

MIKE LUCKOVICH
Courtesy Atlanta Journal-Constitution

CHAN LOWE
Courtesy Fort Lauderdale News/
South Florida Sun Sentinel

MARK BAKER
Courtesy Army Times

BRUCE PLANTE
Courtesy Chattanooga Times

KIRK ANDERSON
Courtesy Lexington Herald-Leader

CLASS WAR

FRANK PAGE
Courtesy Rome Daily Sentinel

MARK BAKER
Courtesy Army Times

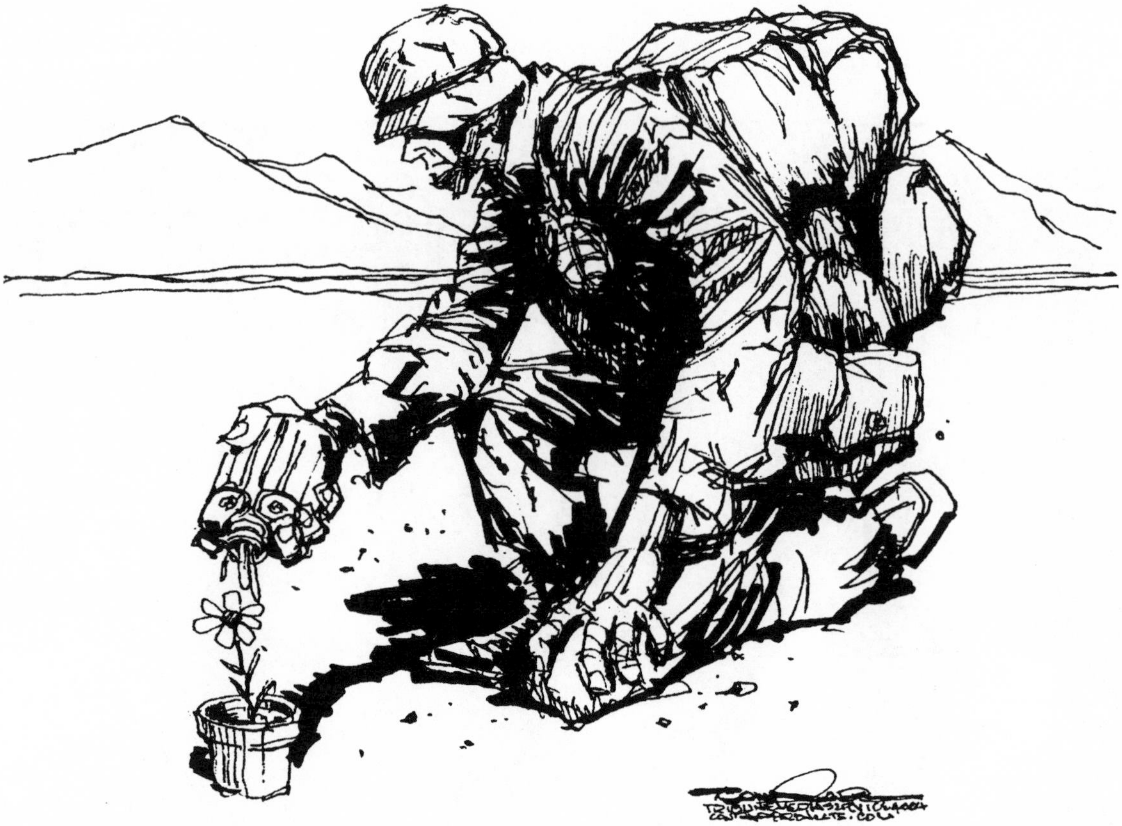

PAUL CONRAD
Courtesy Los Angeles Times Syndicate

DAVE ANDERSON
Courtesy The Beaches Leader

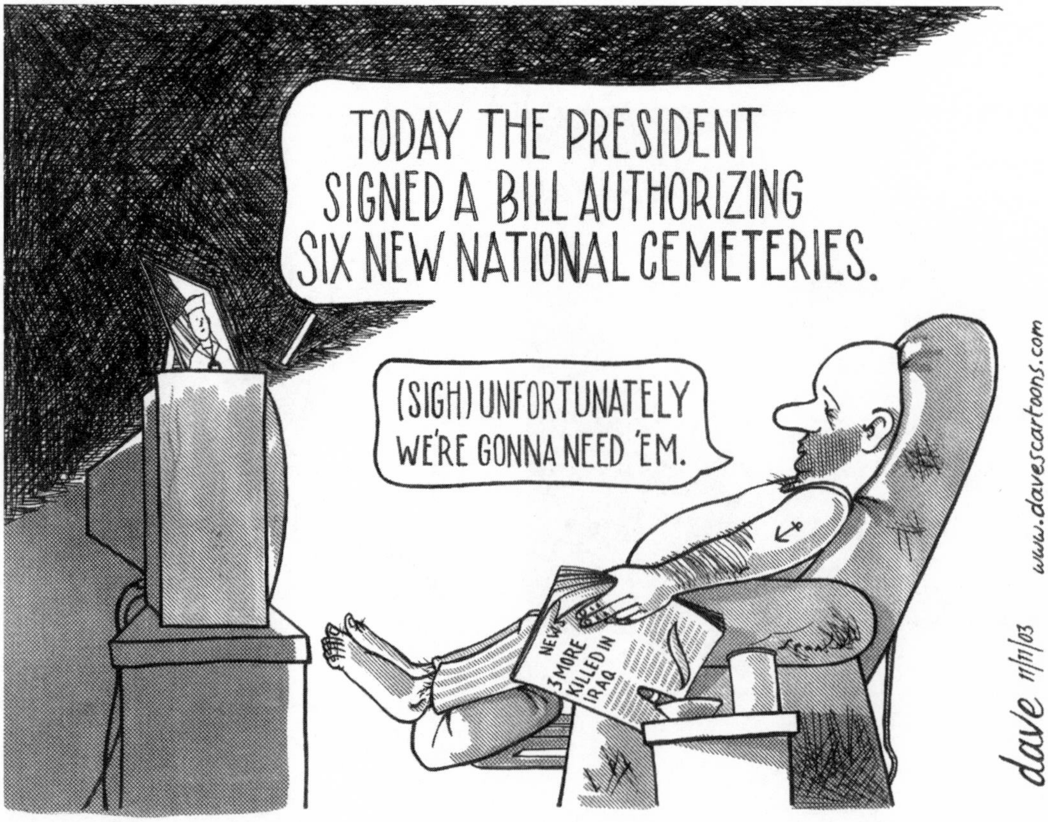
TODAY THE PRESIDENT SIGNED A BILL AUTHORIZING SIX NEW NATIONAL CEMETERIES.
(SIGH) UNFORTUNATELY WE'RE GONNA NEED 'EM.
NEWS 3 MORE KILLED IN IRAQ
www.davescartoons.com
dave 11/11/03

Education

Surveys across the country show that student skills in mathematics and reading are improving and that racial gaps in academic achievement are closing in many states. This broad improvement is attributed by some experts to the No Child Left Behind program of the Bush Administration.

Economists say that a college degree is more critical for good-paying jobs than ever before. Students who work hard and earn good grades can expect to find some scholarship support available to them. States, however, are struggling with budget deficits and are forcing public colleges and universities to make cuts. The institutions in turn are reducing costs by trimming programs and limiting enrollment. 2004 marked the second straight year of large tuition increases. The result is that students are finding it more difficult to get into college.

Because of growing obesity among children, the U.S. Department of Agriculture, which operates the National School Lunch Program, has come under fire. USDA administrators are taking steps to ensure that school food is more nutritious and lower in fat. In addition, more emphasis is being placed on fruit and vegetables.

A ruling by the U.S. Supreme Court apparently says that, for now, the words "under God" will remain in the Pledge of Allegiance.

ED STEIN
Courtesy Rocky Mountain News

149

WHY AMERICANS DON'T READ...

JIM BORGMAN
Courtesy Cincinnati Enquirer

"WELL, YES, WE COULD READ YOUR BLOG.... OR YOU COULD JUST TELL US ABOUT YOUR SCHOOL DAY."

JAMES McCLOSKEY
Courtesy The Daily News Leader (Va.)

TOM BECK
Courtesy Freeport Journal-Standard (Ill.)

DANIEL FENECH
Courtesy Saline Reporter

S. W. PARRA
Courtesy Fresno Bee

JOHN AUCTER
Courtesy Grand Rapids Business Journal

BRUCE QUAST
Courtesy Rockford Register Star (Ill.)

PAM WINTERS
Courtesy North County Times

ROGER SCHILLERSTROM
Courtesy Crain Publications

Society

The controversy over gay marriage made a lot of headlines during the year. After a Massachusetts court ruled that the ban on gay marriages was unconstitutional, the state became the first to permit weddings between members of the same sex. The city of San Francisco, in defiance of California state law, began issuing marriage licenses to same-sex couples.

President Bush joined the fray, calling for a constitutional amendment to bar gay marriage. Similar bans were on the ballot in eleven states in the November elections and all passed by wide margins, indicating a national mood in favor of retaining at least some traditional values.

Every type of violent crime decreased in 2004 except murder, which increased for the fourth straight year. A ban on certain types of assault weapons, signed by President Clinton in 1994, lapsed when Congress did not vote to continue it.

The U.S. Supreme Court ruled that a California atheist could not legally challenge the mention of God in the Pledge of Allegiance because he did not have the authority to speak for his daughter, in whose name he filed the suit.

Adequate funding for Social Security remained one of the top priorities of the Bush Administration's second term.

GARY VARVEL
Courtesy Indianapolis Star

155

RICHARD WALLMEYER
Courtesy Long Beach Press-Telegram

JOHN COLE
Courtesy The Herald-Sun (N.C.)

CHARLES DANIEL
Courtesy Knoxville News-Sentinel

CHIP BOK
Courtesy Akron Beacon Journal

TIM HARTMAN
Courtesy Beaver County Times

TOM BECK
Courtesy Freeport Journal-Standard (Ill.)

PAUL FELL
Courtesy Lincoln Journal Star

ALAN VITELLO
Courtesy Greeley Tribune

STEVE KELLEY
Courtesy The Times-Picayune

ANNETTE BALESTERI
Courtesy Ledger-Dispatch (Calif.)

RICK TUMA
Courtesy Chicago Tribune

LINDA BOILEAU
Courtesy The State Journal (Ky.)

WALT HANDELSMAN
Courtesy Newsday

ED STEIN
Courtesy Rocky Mountain News

WAYNE STAYSKAL
Courtesy Tribune Media Services

LARRY WRIGHT
Courtesy Detroit News

THE WARRIOR IN THE BATTLE FOR THE SANCTITY OF MARRIAGE

PHIL HANDS
Courtesy philtoons.com

JOE MAJESKI
Courtesy The Times-Leader (Pa.)

BILL MANGOLD
Courtesy Heritage Newspapers

ROGER SCHILLERSTROM
Courtesy Crain Publications

"OK, DO YOU WANT TO RISK TERRORISM ON PUBLIC TRANSPORTATION OR RISK HIGHER GAS PRICES AND DRIVE?"

Sports

Threats of terrorist attacks overshadowed the 2004 Olympic Games in Athens. Greece spent $1.7 billion on security measures that were the tightest ever for the Olympics. More than 70,000 Greek police officers and soldiers patrolled sporting events. The investment apparently paid off as no incidents of violence occurred. The U.S. led in medals with 103, but America's men's basketball team suffered a stunning defeat.

The Boston Red Sox made it to the World Series after trailing New York in the playoff series three games to zero. The Sox went on to capture the World Series in four straight games. It was their first championship since 1918, thus erasing a "curse" put on the team for having traded the immortal Babe Ruth to New York early in his career.

The use of performance-enhancing drugs by athletes continued to plague sports, especially at the professional level. Near year's end, some of sports' greatest figures allegedly admitted in grand jury testimony to having used steroids. Sen. John McCain announced that if Major League Baseball did not put its house in order on the illegal drug question, Congress would.

In his autobiography, baseball great Pete Rose admitted to having placed bets on baseball games.

JOSEPH F. O'MAHONEY
Courtesy The Patriot Ledger

MICKEY SIPORIN
Courtesy The Westsider

JOE HOFFECKER
Courtesy American City Business Journals

JOE MAJESKI
Courtesy The Times-Leader (Pa.)

PLAY BALL!

J. Thornhill Lawrence County Record

JOEL THORNHILL
Courtesy Lawrence County Record

STEVE BREEN
Courtesy San Diego Union-Tribune

JOHN SHERFFIUS
Courtesy jsherffius@aol.com

VIC HARVILLE
Courtesy Stephens Media Group

DANA SUMMERS
Courtesy Orlando Sentinel

J. R. ROSE
Courtesy Byrd Newspapers

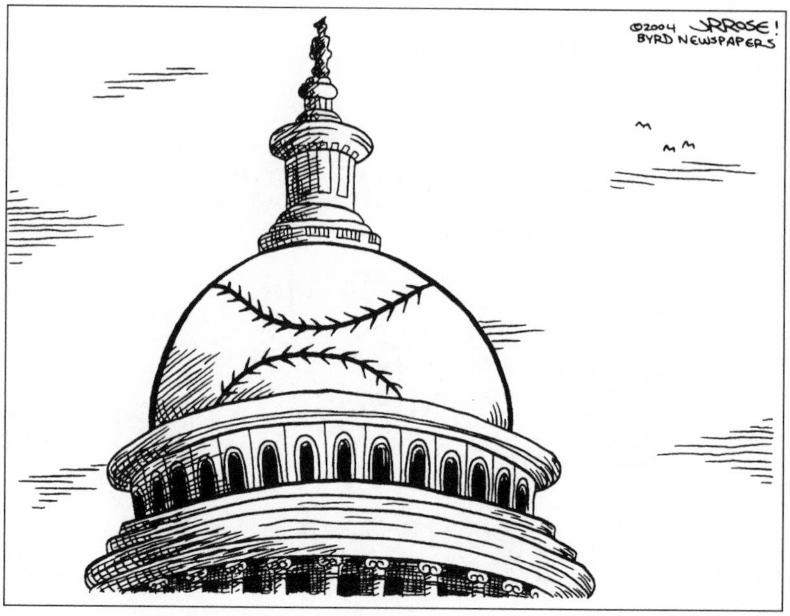
©2004 JRROSE!
BYRD NEWSPAPERS

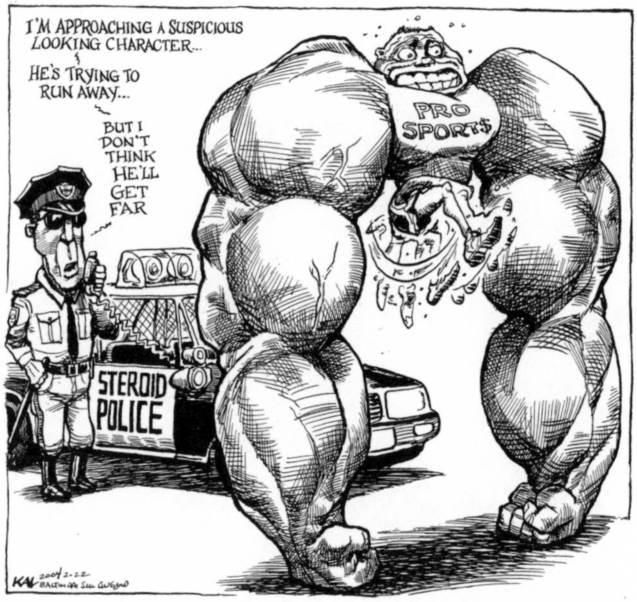
I'M APPROACHING A SUSPICIOUS LOOKING CHARACTER...
HE'S TRYING TO RUN AWAY...
BUT I DON'T THINK HE'LL GET FAR
PRO SPORT$
STEROID POLICE

KEVIN KALLAUGHER
Courtesy Baltimore Sun

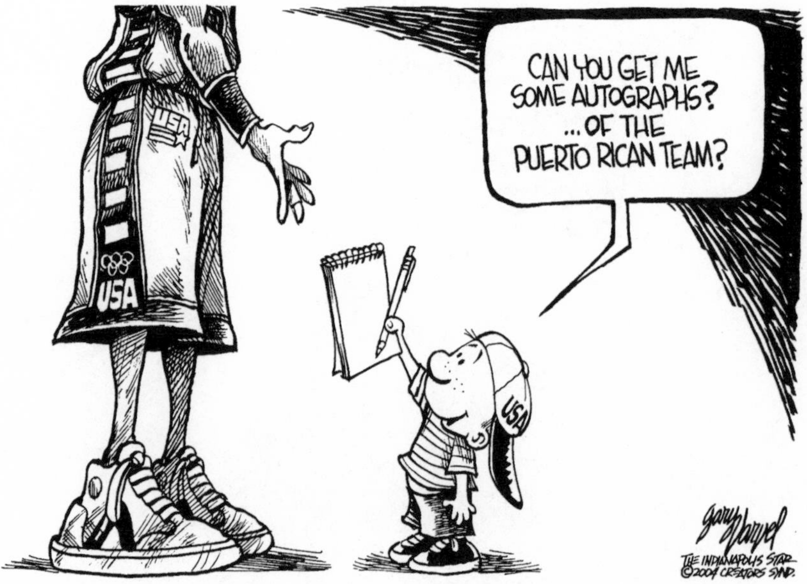
CAN YOU GET ME SOME AUTOGRAPHS? ...OF THE PUERTO RICAN TEAM?
USA
USA
USA
THE INDIANAPOLIS STAR ©2004 CREATORS SYND.

GARY VARVEL
Courtesy Indianapolis Star

DANIEL FENECH
Courtesy Saline Reporter

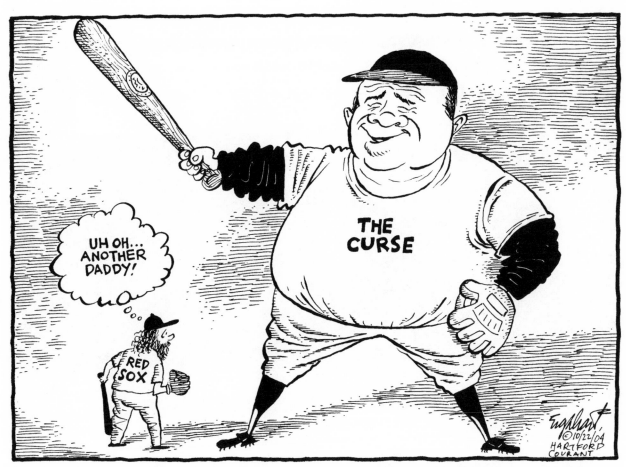

BOB ENGLEHART
Courtesy Hartford Courant

WILLIAM FLINT
Courtesy Dallas Morning News

As the first color images come back from the surface of Mars, the question of its ability to sustain life may soon be answered.

DAVE SATTLER
Courtesy Lafayette Journal and Courier

Space / Air Travel

SpaceShipOne, a privately funded space vehicle, climbed to an altitude of 71½ miles to win the $10 million Ansari X Prize. The X Prize was established as an incentive for privately funded, non-governmental groups to build a spacecraft that could carry three adults to an altitude of 62 miles twice in fourteen days. More than twenty teams entered the competition.

NASA's Mars rover Spirit landed on the red planet on January 3 and began sending back stunning images. President Bush announced a new space initiative rivaling the race to the moon. He wants to establish on the moon's surface a permanent colony that would be used as a base to send a spacecraft to Mars.

A NASA project went awry when the Genesis space capsule slammed into the Utah desert after its parachutes failed, leaving scientists unsure whether its cargo of solar dust had survived the journey to Earth. NASA had hoped the microscopic particles would help them better understand how the sun and planets were formed.

Some airlines remained on the brink financially. Delta warned it would probably have to file for bankruptcy. ATA Airlines, the nation's tenth largest air carrier, filed for bankruptcy in October.

BRUCE PLANTE
Courtesy Chattanooga Times

ERIC SMITH
Courtesy Annapolis Capital-Gazette

TIM DOLIGHAN
Courtesy Toronto Sun

JIMMY MARGULIES
Courtesy The Record (N.J.)

174

DOUG MacGREGOR
Courtesy Fort Myers News-Press

WAYNE STAYSKAL
Courtesy Tribune Media Services

175

JIMMY MARGULIES
Courtesy The Record (N.J.)

G. MARTY STEIN
Courtesy LaPrensa

"THE FUTURE OF SPACE TOURISM ..."   "WELCOME TO THE MAGIC KINGDOM OF THE MOON"

Canada

The Liberal Party lost outright control of Parliament in a June election but easily won the largest share of seats. Though dogged by scandal and pressed by a newly unified Conservative Party, the Liberals prevailed by holding their ground in Ontario, the most populous province. In Quebec, the Bloc Quebecois, which advocates independence for the French-speaking province, did well at the Liberals' expense.

Former Prime Minister Jean Chretien was linked to a $250 million sponsorship scandal, dubbed Abscam. It was alleged that Chretien had a part in approving funding for costly public relations efforts. A memo surfaced in which a senior bureaucrat said that $450,000 for a 20-part television series called "Tradewinds" would have to await approval from the prime minister's office. It was speculated that current Prime Minister Paul Martin might also be involved since he was finance minister at the time.

After years of battling illegal and costly U.S. tariffs, Canada won a NAFTA decision over the softwood lumber lobby. Great Britain sold Canada four submarines, one of which was later involved in an accident in which one officer was killed and several seamen injured.

TIM DOLIGHAN
Courtesy Toronto Sun

ROY PETERSON
Courtesy Vancouver Sun

TIM DOLIGHAN
Courtesy Toronto Sun

ROY PETERSON
Courtesy Vancouver Sun

MALCOLM MAYES
Courtesy Edmonton Journal

TIM DOLIGHAN
Courtesy Toronto Sun

ROY PETERSON
Courtesy Vancouver Sun

The Driver of the Getaway Car

ROY PETERSON
Courtesy Vancouver Sun

TIM DOLIGHAN
Courtesy Toronto Sun

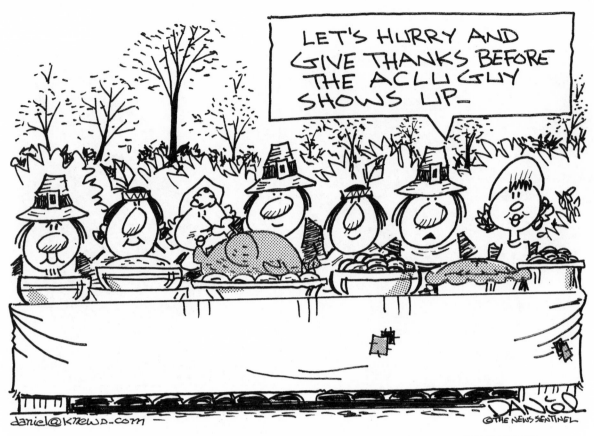

CHARLES DANIEL
Courtesy Knoxville News-Sentinel

RICK KOLLINGER
Courtesy The Star-Democrat (Md.)

. . . and Other Issues

Following a lengthy study of the terrorist attack on 9/11, the 9/11 Commission issued a report criticizing the CIA, concluding that the U.S. was unprepared to deal with terrorism and that Congress was guilty of inaction. CIA Director George Tenet resigned amid calls for immediate intelligence reforms.

A jury found domestic icon Martha Stewart guilty of obstruction of justice, making false statements, and conspiracy to obstruct justice. She began serving a five-month sentence in October. A federal court ruled that former Enron Corporation Chairman Ken Lay should be tried alongside fellow executives Jeffrey Skilling and Richard Causey on charges linked to the energy company's collapse.

President Bush was bombarded with criticism for not presenting a plan to adequately control the nation's borders against illegal aliens. Incidentally, the national deficit continued to grow to record levels.

Former President Bill Clinton underwent successful heart surgery and Ronald Reagan died at the age of 93. Other notables who died in 2004 included Jack Paar, Ray Charles, Rodney Dangerfield, Bob Keeshan, Ann Miller, Christopher Reeve, Tony Randall, and Marlon Brando.

S. W. PARRA
Courtesy Fresno Bee

**Ronald Reagan
1911 - 2004**

ROGER HARVELL
Courtesy Greenville News-Piedmont

PAUL BERGE
Courtesy Racine Journal-Times

STEVE KELLEY
Courtesy The Times-Picayune

ETTA HULME
Courtesy Fort Worth Star-Telegram

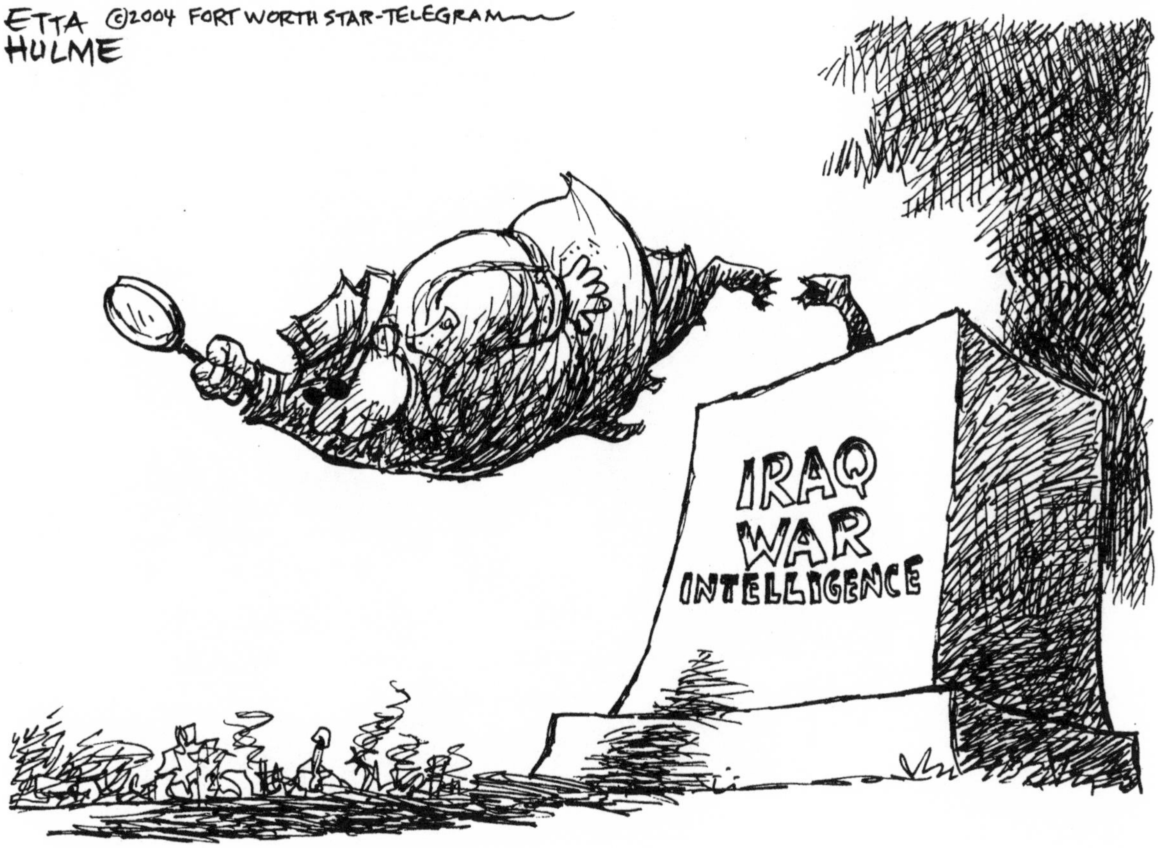
ETTA HULME ©2004 FORT WORTH STAR-TELEGRAM
IRAQ WAR INTELLIGENCE

GARY MARKSTEIN
Courtesy Milwaukee Journal Sentinel

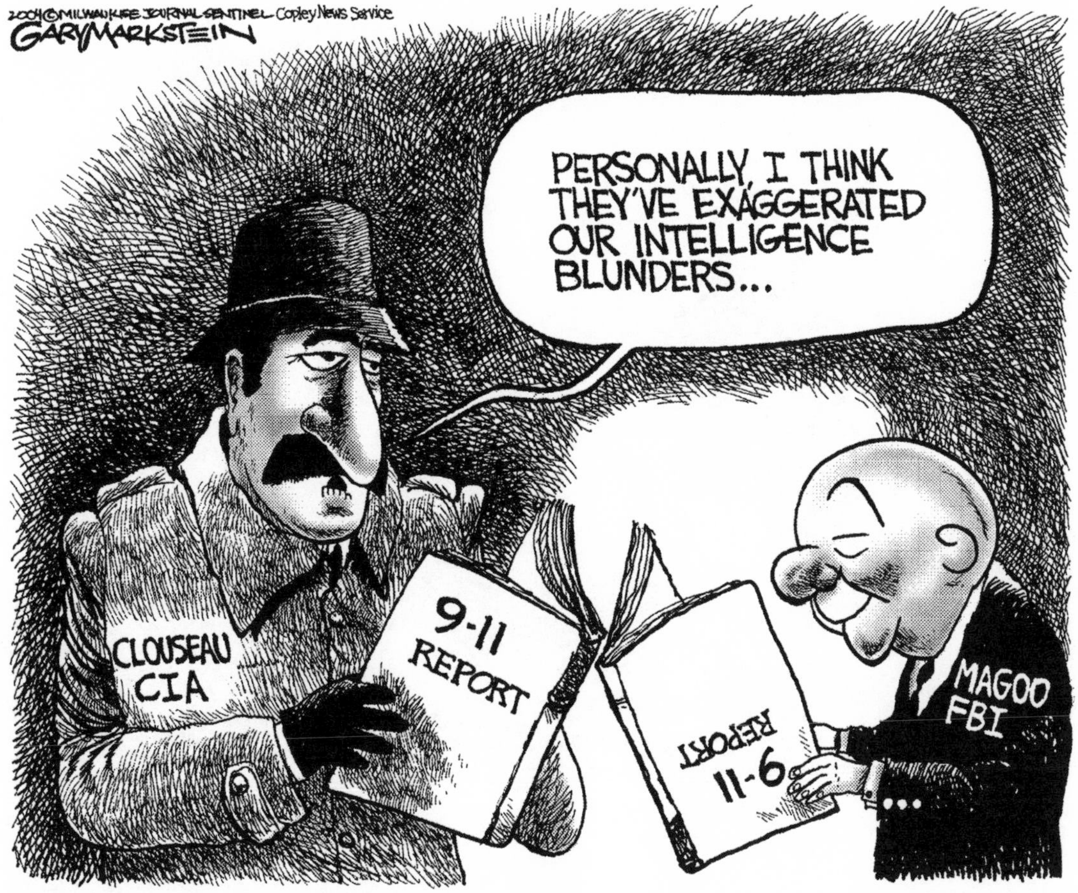
2004 © MILWAUKEE JOURNAL SENTINEL Copley News Service GARY MARKSTEIN
PERSONALLY, I THINK THEY'VE EXAGGERATED OUR INTELLIGENCE BLUNDERS...
CLOUSEAU CIA
9-11 REPORT
MAGOO FBI

MIKE PETERS
Courtesy Dayton Daily News

ROGER HARVELL
Courtesy Greenville News-Piedmont

JONATHAN TODD
Courtesy Shreveport Times

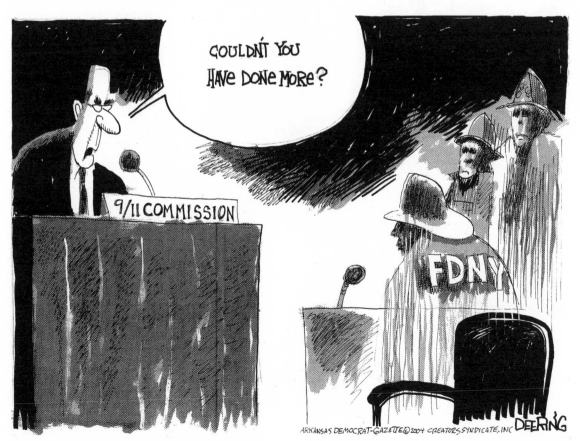

JOHN DEERING
Courtesy Arkansas Democrat-Gazette

ED COLLEY
Courtesy Boston Globe South/Northwest

There's no place like home.

ED GAMBLE
Courtesy Florida Times-Union

REX BABIN
Courtesy Sacramento Bee

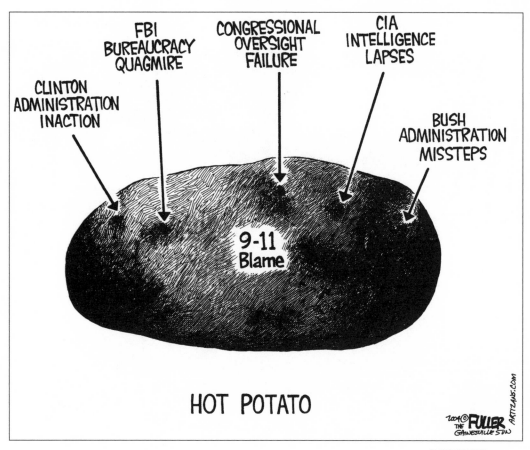

JAKE FULLER
Courtesy Gainesville Sun

CHRIS BRITT
Courtesy State Journal-Register

CLAY JONES
Courtesy Free Lance-Star (Va.)

THE WORLD REACTS TO THE 5-MONTH JAIL SENTENCE OF THE DOMESTIC DIVA-

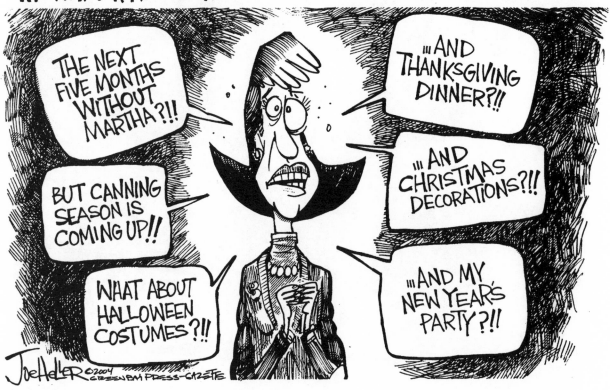

JOE HELLER
Courtesy Green Bay Press-Gazette

CORPORATE FASHION UPDATE

ORANGE JUMPSUIT

ORANGE SWIMSUIT

GARY MARKSTEIN
Courtesy Milwaukee Journal Sentinel

MIKE PETERS
Courtesy Dayton Daily News

GERALD GARDEN
Courtesy UTP Voice

BILL SMITH
Courtesy Lompoc Record (Calif.)

MIKE KEEFE
Courtesy Denver Post

ED STEIN
Courtesy Rocky Mountain News

MALCOLM MAYES
Courtesy Edmonton Journal

RANDY BISH
Courtesy Tribune-Review (Pa.)

JOE HOFFECKER
Courtesy American City Business Journals

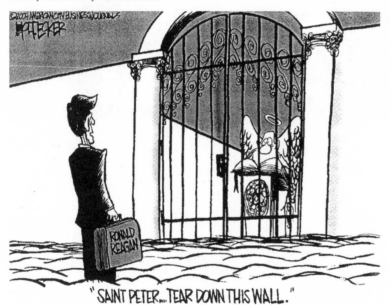

BOB UNELL
Courtesy Kansas City Star

CHIP BOK
Courtesy Akron Beacon Journal

JERRY BARNETT
Courtesy Indianapolis Star

PETER EVANS
Courtesy Islander News

BILL GARNER
Courtesy Washington Times

FAREWELL

GLENN FODEN
Courtesy Patuxent Publishing Company

194

CHUCK ASAY
Courtesy Colorado Springs Gazette-Telegraph

CLAY JONES
Courtesy Free Lance-Star (Va.)

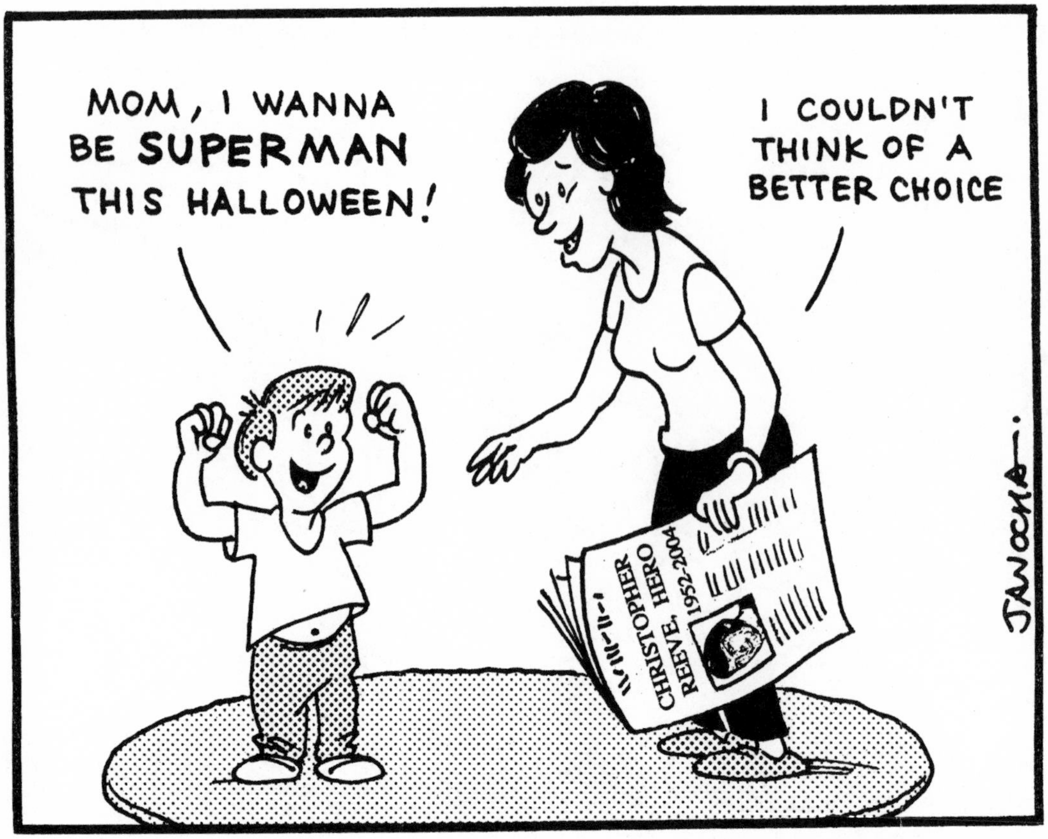
MOM, I WANNA BE SUPERMAN THIS HALLOWEEN!
I COULDN'T THINK OF A BETTER CHOICE
CHRISTOPHER REEVE, HERO 1952-2004
JANOCHA

BILL JANOCHA
Courtesy Greenwich Times

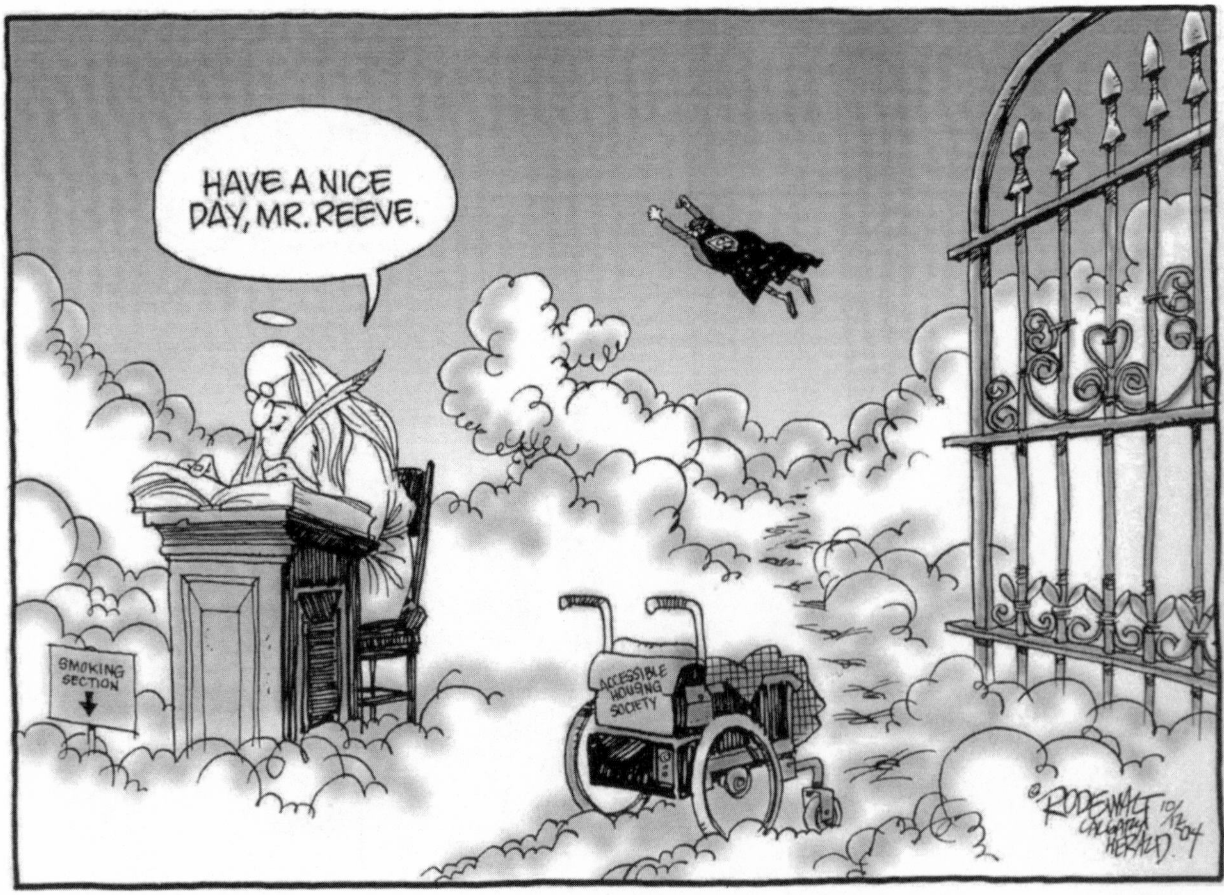
HAVE A NICE DAY, MR. REEVE.
SMOKING SECTION
ACCESSIBLE HOUSING SOCIETY
© RODEWALT 10/12/04 CALGARY HERALD

VANCE RODEWALT
Courtesy Calgary Herald

STEVE BREEN
Courtesy San Diego Union-Tribune

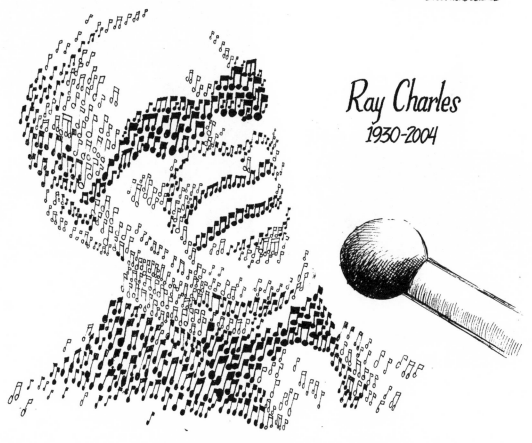

Ray Charles
1930-2004

J. D. CROWE
Courtesy Mobile Register

"FATHER OF SOUL"

RAY CHARLES
1930-2004

10 years later...

O.J. is still looking
for the killers.

DAVID G. BROWN
Courtesy Los Angeles Sentinel

BILL VALLADARES
Courtesy Montclair Times

JOE KING
Courtesy Santa Monica Daily Press

VANCE RODEWALT
Courtesy Calgary Herald

THEN-
Lone Eagle: Super Power!

NOW-
Lonely Eagle: Suffer'd Power

© 2004 FILIPINO REPORTER, NY City

DANI AGUILA
Courtesy Filipino Reporter

MATT DAVIES
Courtesy The Journal News (N.Y.)

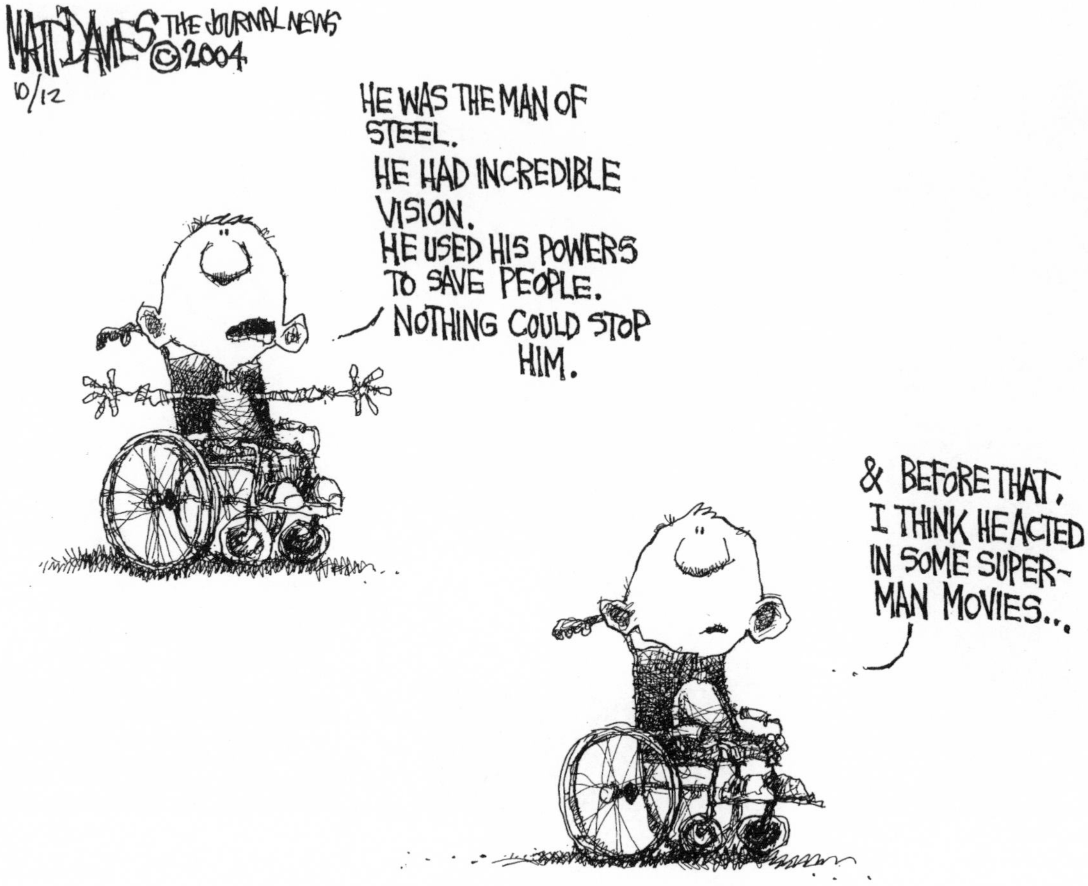
MATT DAVIES THE JOURNAL NEWS ©2004
10/12
HE WAS THE MAN OF STEEL. HE HAD INCREDIBLE VISION. HE USED HIS POWERS TO SAVE PEOPLE. NOTHING COULD STOP HIM.
& BEFORE THAT, I THINK HE ACTED IN SOME SUPER-MAN MOVIES...

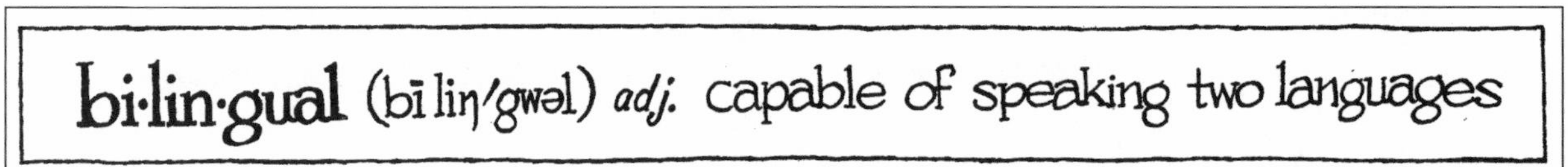
bi·lin·gual (bī liŋ/gwəl) adj. capable of speaking two languages
GO HOME!
BUT FIRST, FINISH HARVESTING MY FOOD, CLEANING MY HOUSE AND MOWING MY LAWN.
BREEN San Diego Union-Tribune © 1-8-04
COPLEY NEWS SERVICE

STEVE BREEN
Courtesy San Diego Union-Tribune

ANN CLEAVES
Courtesy Palisadian Post

LARRY WRIGHT
Courtesy Detroit News

STEVEN LAIT
Courtesy Oakland Tribune

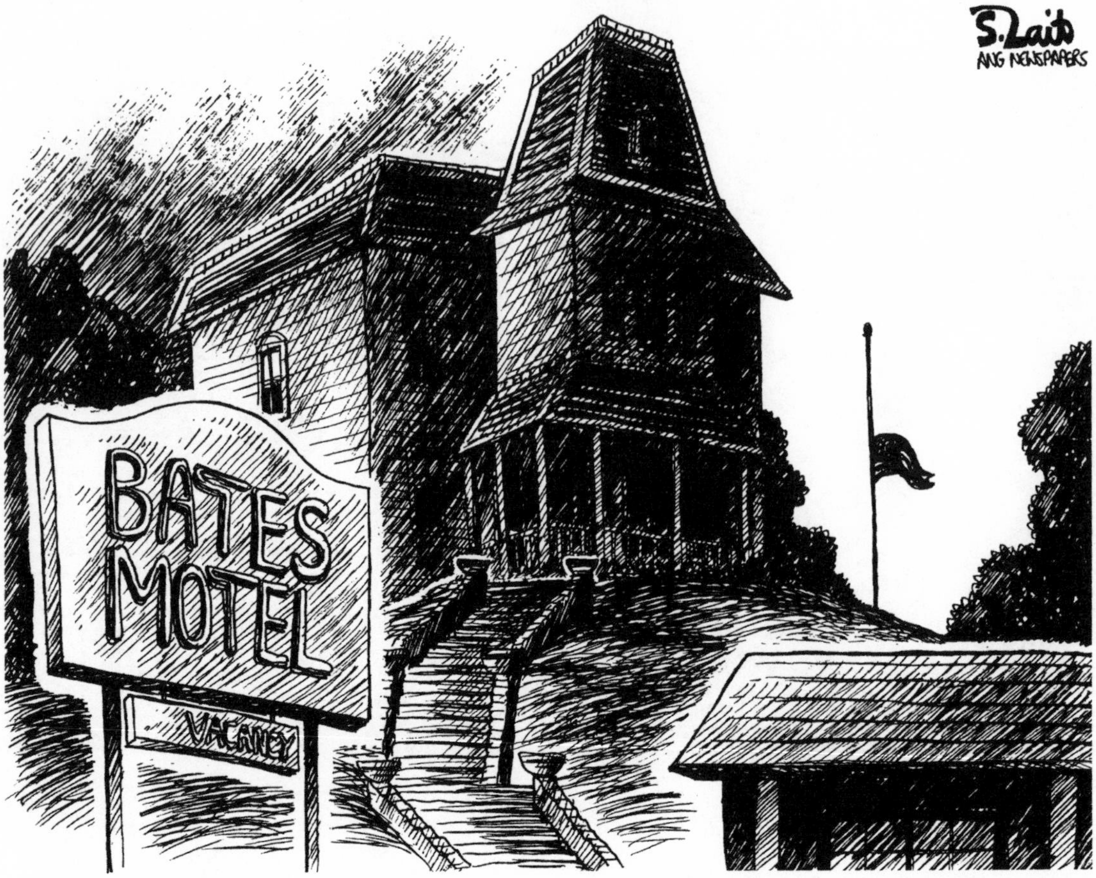
S. Lait
ANG NEWSPAPERS
BATES MOTEL
VACANCY

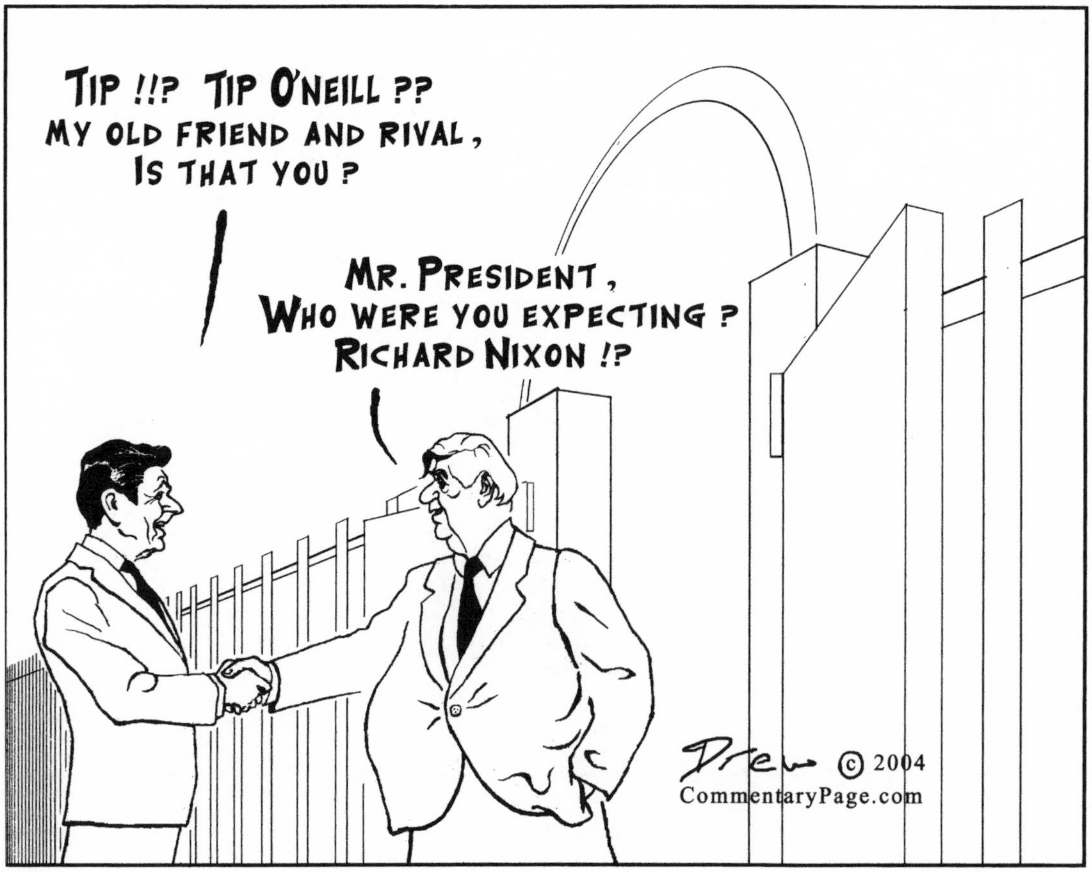
TIP !!? TIP O'NEILL ?? MY OLD FRIEND AND RIVAL, IS THAT YOU ?
MR. PRESIDENT, WHO WERE YOU EXPECTING ? RICHARD NIXON !?
Drew © 2004
CommentaryPage.com

DREW CHAPMAN
Courtesy CommentaryPage.com

Past Award Winners

PULITZER PRIZE

1922—Rollin Kirby, New York World
1923—No award given
1924—J.N. Darling, New York Herald-Tribune
1925—Rollin Kirby, New York World
1926—D.R. Fitzpatrick, St. Louis Post-Dispatch
1927—Nelson Harding, Brooklyn Eagle
1928—Nelson Harding, Brooklyn Eagle
1929—Rollin Kirby, New York World
1930—Charles Macauley, Brooklyn Eagle
1931—Edmund Duffy, Baltimore Sun
1932—John T. McCutcheon, Chicago Tribune
1933—H.M. Talburt, Washington Daily News
1934—Edmund Duffy, Baltimore Sun
1935—Ross A. Lewis, Milwaukee Journal
1936—No award given
1937—C.D. Batchelor, New York Daily News
1938—Vaughn Shoemaker, Chicago Daily News
1939—Charles G. Werner, Daily Oklahoman
1940—Edmund Duffy, Baltimore Sun
1941—Jacob Burck, Chicago Times
1942—Herbert L. Block, NEA
1943—Jay N. Darling, New York Herald-Tribune
1944—Clifford K. Berryman, Washington Star
1945—Bill Mauldin, United Features Syndicate
1946—Bruce Russell, Los Angeles Times
1947—Vaughn Shoemaker, Chicago Daily News
1948—Reuben L. ("Rube") Goldberg, New York Sun
1949—Lute Pease, Newark Evening News
1950—James T. Berryman, Washington Star
1951—Reginald W. Manning, Arizona Republic
1952—Fred L. Packer, New York Mirror
1953—Edward D. Kuekes, Cleveland Plain Dealer
1954—Herbert L. Block, Washington Post
1955—Daniel R. Fitzpatrick, St. Louis Post-Dispatch
1956—Robert York, Louisville Times
1957—Tom Little, Nashville Tennessean
1958—Bruce M. Shanks, Buffalo Evening News
1959—Bill Mauldin, St. Louis Post-Dispatch
1960—No award given
1961—Carey Orr, Chicago Tribune
1962—Edmund S. Valtman, Hartford Times
1963—Frank Miller, Des Moines Register
1964—Paul Conrad, Denver Post
1965—No award given
1966—Don Wright, Miami News
1967—Patrick B. Oliphant, Denver Post
1968—Eugene Gray Payne, Charlotte Observer
1969—John Fischetti, Chicago Daily News
1970—Thomas F. Darcy, Newsday
1971—Paul Conrad, Los Angeles Times
1972—Jeffrey K. MacNelly, Richmond News Leader
1973—No award given
1974—Paul Szep, Boston Globe

1975—Garry Trudeau, Universal Press Syndicate
1976—Tony Auth, Philadelphia Enquirer
1977—Paul Szep, Boston Globe
1978—Jeff MacNelly, Richmond News Leader
1979—Herbert Block, Washington Post
1980—Don Wright, Miami News
1981—Mike Peters, Dayton Daily News
1982—Ben Sargent, Austin American-Statesman
1983—Dick Locher, Chicago Tribune
1984—Paul Conrad, Los Angeles Times
1985—Jeff MacNelly, Chicago Tribune
1986—Jules Feiffer, Universal Press Syndicate
1987—Berke Breathed, Washington Post Writers Group
1988—Doug Marlette, Atlanta Constitution
1989—Jack Higgins, Chicago Sun-Times
1990—Tom Toles, Buffalo News
1991—Jim Borgman, Cincinnati Enquirer
1992—Signe Wilkinson, Philadelphia Daily News
1993—Steve Benson, Arizona Republic
1994—Michael Ramirez, Memphis Commercial Appeal
1995—Mike Luckovich, Atlanta Constitution
1996—Jim Morin, Miami Herald
1997—Walt Handelsman, New Orleans Times-Picayune
1998—Steve Breen, Asbury Park Press
1999—David Horsey, Seattle Post-Intelligencer
2000—Joel Pett, Lexington Herald-Leader
2001—Ann Telnaes, Tribune Media Services
2002—Clay Bennett, Christian Science Monitor
2003—David Horsey, Seattle Post-Intelligencer
2004—Matt Davies, The Journal News

NATIONAL SOCIETY OF PROFESSIONAL JOURNALISTS AWARD (SIGMA DELTA CHI AWARD)

1942—Jacob Burck, Chicago Times
1943—Charles Werner, Chicago Sun
1944—Henry Barrow, Associated Press
1945—Reuben L. Goldberg, New York Sun
1946—Dorman H. Smith, NEA
1947—Bruce Russell, Los Angeles Times
1948—Herbert Block, Washington Post
1949—Herbert Block, Washington Post
1950—Bruce Russell, Los Angeles Times
1951—Herbert Block, Washington Post and
       Bruce Russell, Los Angeles Times
1952—Cecil Jensen, Chicago Daily News
1953—John Fischetti, NEA
1954—Calvin Alley, Memphis Commercial Appeal
1955—John Fischetti, NEA
1956—Herbert Block, Washington Post
1957—Scott Long, Minneapolis Tribune

PAST AWARD WINNERS

1958—Clifford H. Baldowski, Atlanta Constitution
1959—Charles G. Brooks, Birmingham News
1960—Dan Dowling, New York Herald-Tribune
1961—Frank Interlandi, Des Moines Register
1962—Paul Conrad, Denver Post
1963—William Mauldin, Chicago Sun-Times
1964—Charles Bissell, Nashville Tennessean
1965—Roy Justus, Minneapolis Star
1966—Patrick Oliphant, Denver Post
1967—Eugene Payne, Charlotte Observer
1968—Paul Conrad, Los Angeles Times
1969—William Mauldin, Chicago Sun-Times
1970—Paul Conrad, Los Angeles Times
1971—Hugh Haynie, Louisville Courier-Journal
1972—William Mauldin, Chicago Sun-Times
1973—Paul Szep, Boston Globe
1974—Mike Peters, Dayton Daily News
1975—Tony Auth, Philadelphia Enquirer
1976—Paul Szep, Boston Globe
1977—Don Wright, Miami News
1978—Jim Borgman, Cincinnati Enquirer
1979—John P. Trever, Albuquerque Journal
1980—Paul Conrad, Los Angeles Times

1981—Paul Conrad, Los Angeles Times
1982—Dick Locher, Chicago Tribune
1983—Rob Lawlor, Philadelphia Daily News
1984—Mike Lane, Baltimore Evening Sun
1985—Doug Marlette, Charlotte Observer
1986—Mike Keefe, Denver Post
1987—Paul Conrad, Los Angeles Times
1988—Jack Higgins, Chicago Sun-Times
1989—Don Wright, Palm Beach Post
1990—Jeff MacNelly, Chicago Tribune
1991—Walt Handelsman, New Orleans Times-Picayune
1992—Robert Ariail, Columbia State
1993—Herbert Block, Washington Post
1994—Jim Borgman, Cincinnati Enquirer
1995—Michael Ramirez, Memphis Commercial Appeal
1996—Paul Conrad, Los Angeles Times
1997—Michael Ramirez, Los Angeles Times
1998—Jack Higgins, Chicago Sun-Times
1999—Mike Thompson, Detroit Free Press
2000—Nick Anderson, Louisville Courier-Journal
2001—Clay Bennett, Christian Science Monitor
2002—Mike Thompson, Detroit Free Press
2003—Steve Sack, Minneapolis Star-Tribune

Index of Cartoonists

INDEX OF CARTOONISTS

Complete Your
CARTOON COLLECTION

Previous editions of this timeless classic are available for those wishing to update their collection of the most provocative moments of the past three decades. In the early days the topics were the oil crisis, Richard Nixon's presidency, Watergate, and the Vietnam War. Those subjects have given way to the Clinton impeachment trial, the historic 2000 presidential election, and the terrorist attack on America. Most important, in the end, the wit and wisdom of the editorial cartoonists prevail on the pages of these op-ed editorials, where one can find memories and much, much more in the work of the nation's finest cartoonists.

Select from the following supply of past editions

_____ 1972 Edition $18.95 pb (F)	_____ 1985 Edition $18.95 pb (F)	_____ 1997 Edition $14.95 pb
_____ 1974 Edition $18.95 pb (F)	_____ 1986 Edition $18.95 pb (F)	_____ 1998 Edition $14.95 pb
_____ 1975 Edition $18.95 pb (F)	_____ 1987 Edition $14.95 pb	_____ 1999 Edition $14.95 pb
_____ 1976 Edition $18.95 pb (F)	_____ 1988 Edition $14.95 pb	_____ 2000 Edition $14.95 pb
_____ 1977 Edition $18.95 pb (F)	_____ 1989 Edition $18.95 pb (F)	_____ 2001 Edition $14.95 pb
_____ 1978 Edition $18.95 pb (F)	_____ 1990 Edition $14.95 pb	_____ 2002 Edition $14.95 pb
_____ 1979 Edition $18.95 pb (F)	_____ 1991 Edition $14.95 pb	_____ 2003 Edition $14.95 pb
_____ 1980 Edition $18.95 pb (F)	_____ 1992 Edition $14.95 pb	_____ 2004 Edition $14.95 pb
_____ 1981 Edition $18.95 pb (F)	_____ 1993 Edition $14.95 pb	_____ 2005 Edition $14.95 pb
_____ 1982 Edition $18.95 pb (F)	_____ 1994 Edition $14.95 pb	_____ Add me to the list of standing
_____ 1983 Edition $18.95 pb (F)	_____ 1995 Edition $14.95 pb	orders
_____ 1984 Edition $18.95 pb (F)	_____ 1996 Edition $14.95 pb	

Please include $2.75 for 4th Class Postage and handling or $5.35 for UPS Ground Shipment plus $.75 for each additional copy ordered.

Total enclosed: _____

NAME_____

ADDRESS _____

CITY_____STATE_____ZIP_____

Make checks payable to:

PELICAN PUBLISHING COMPANY
P.O. Box 3110, Dept. 6BEC
Gretna, Louisiana 70054-3110

CREDIT CARD ORDERS CALL 1-800-843-1724 or or go to e-pelican.com/store
Jefferson Parish residents add 8¾% tax. All other Louisiana residents add 4% tax.
Please visit our Web site at www.pelicanpub.com or e-mail us at sales@pelicanpub.com